THE
RICH
LABOURER

ALSO BY PARTHAJEET SARMA

Smart Phones, Dumb People?

Version 1: 2017

All rights reserved. No part of this book may be used or reproduced in any manner whatsoever without written permission from the authors.

ATTENTION: ORGANISATIONS & INSTITUTIONS
- This book is available at quantity discounts for bulk purchases with corporate branding if necessary.
- The methodology described in the book is also delivered through talks and workshops.

For information, please email: trl@idream.in

THE
RICH
LABOURER

A 3-step path to finding solutions; for people, organisations and for society.

By Parthajeet Sarma

Co-authoured by Sibani Sarma

About the authors

Parthajeet Sarma (B.Arch., MBA): Entrepreneur and founder of innovation consultancy iDream, Parthajeet is a Chevening fellow (Oxford Univ, UK). He not only consults organisations at a strategic level, but spends ample time on internal R&D efforts, which has led to award winning products and services, especially around mass housing.

Also by Parthajeet: "Smart Phones Dumb People?" Available on Amazon.

You can connect with Parthajeet at:
- parthajeet@parthajeet.com
- www.Parthajeet.com
- www.idream.in

Sibani Sarma (B.Arch, MBA): With a research background spanning across large conglomerates, Sibani is the founder of skill development & capacity building firm Gallopper. She aides landowners conceptualise realistic business models based on a Viability-Feasibility-Desirability approach. She also enables training and skill development for students and white collared professionals.

You can connect with Sibani at:
- sibani.sarma@Gallopper.com
- www.linkedin.com/in/sibanisarma
- www.Gallopper.com

To the human in you.

CONTENTS

	Introduction	11
1.	The 3P method	15
2.	Defining the problem	33
3.	Mapping the journey	49
4.	Doing it	65
5.	Sustainability	77
6.	Inspiration	87
7.	The 3P method in organisations	95
8.	Designing experiences	109
9.	For a better self	117
10.	For society	129
	Conclusion	141

Introduction

Mary is a young and beautiful princess. She will rule her land one day and like in most monarchies, may remain Queen till her old age. She will traverse this path over fifty-sixty years, till she has wrinkled skin.

Fifty-sixty years? Want to see some magic? Well, turn this book upside down now.

Surprised? Mary turned into an eighty year old in one second. This is about perspective. The same thing can appear different from different angles. The same thing may mean different things to different people.

The Rich Labourer

Unless one accepts this as a fact of life, one is likely to upset a lot of people in one's day-to-day lives. The products that can be sold to a twenty year old Mary are very different from the products, which can be sold to an eighty year old Mary. People go wrong in interpersonal relationships due to this Mary syndrome. Product manufacturers sometimes sell the wrong products to the wrong target group due to unclear understanding of the user's needs. Governments are seen to fail in attempts to fix socio-economic problems due to a lack of understanding of the people's perspective.

In problem solving, it is critical that the perspective of people for who the solution is meant, is clearly understood. This is only possible if one is able to put oneself in the shoes of the other. The ability to do that is empathy.

Who is Mary? Is she twenty or is she eighty? What are her likes and her dislikes? To which social strata does she belong? What motivates her? Empathy allows one to be human centric. Path breaking solutions emerge only when the 'human' behind people are understood; when desirability is given equal, if not higher, status, than feasibility and viability.

In innovation driven initiatives, there is a tendency to quickly jump to a solution without first getting the problem clearly defined. Without developing empathy for end users, one often ends up finding solutions for wrongly defined problems. This tends to further complicate things or ends up being a waste of time and money.

Organisations and society can save millions of dollars by not rushing into a solution. People can save themselves a lot of trouble by not allowing quick-fix solutions. Was the demonetization of high value Indian currency bills a quick-fix solution or a well thought-through program to address socio-economic malaises? There is a structured way towards finding solutions; in three simple steps. This book is an attempt to make this process simple. To make the process easy-to-understand, the book is written with a fictional story in the background, sprinkled with facts.

Co-create this Book

At the core of the mentioned three steps, is the powerful impact of co-creating solutions. The publication of this book itself follows a co-creation methodology. True value of any product or service is co-created with the end-user, and not otherwise. What you have in your hands is the first version of the book. The authors wish to open-source the contents for the next version of the book. Version 2 is expected to be an improved version based upon readers' contributions. You are encouraged to leave your comments and feedback on how the book can be enhanced in terms of contents. Your feedback will be utilized to re-write the new version; due credits will be given.

The Rich Labourer

Kindly use the following link to contribute to Version 2:

www.Parthajeet.com/TheRichLabourer/

It may make sense to have a pencil with you while reading the book, so that you can make notes.

Let's begin at the beginning…

1

The 3P method

"Maa, my legs are gone!" Seema screamed, as Saee turned towards her, startled.

Saee saw Seema crying, huddled in the corner of the only bed in the room, as she looked in dismay at the paper in her hand. The roof was leaking again, and a drop of water had fallen on the sketch that Seema was working on for the last thirty minutes. She had made a sketch of her family, which comprised of her father Ramesh, Saee, and her five year old, younger brother, Rohit; all standing in front of what looked like a brightly painted pink house.

The Rich Labourer

Seema had been working with water-colours; and the water drop had fallen on the lower part of her own caricature in the sketch. She tried to rub it off, and in the process had almost erased her legs off the sketch. The watercolour set was a partly used one, and given to Seema by Riya in whose house Saee worked as a maid.

"Let it dry; don't do anything now." Saee cajoled Seema, as she got up from washing the dishes and came towards Seema, who was sitting next to a sleeping Rohit, on the bed. She took the sketch from Seema, dabbed a corner of her saree carefully on the spots where water had fallen, and carefully kept it on top of the TV set. It was an old box like TV set that Saee had got from Riya five years ago, and which also doubled up as a table top in the 10' x 10' room in the Andheri West slums that they lived in. It was connected to a satellite dish that was fixed on the external wall near the door to the room. The plastic moulded door was at the top end of a flight of steps from the ground level.

Ramesh was a construction worker, and was out for the day on a site. Six years back, when Seema was two, Ramesh had decided to move to Mumbai from a village called Shikrapur near Pune, in search of better opportunities for the family. Initially he had moved alone, and after a year, he got Saee and Seema to relocate as well. Rohit was born in Mumbai. The room they occupied was on rent, and they paid three thousand rupees a month to the landlord, Subhash.

The Rich Labourer

The room was on the first floor of a structure in the Anand Nagar slums at Andheri West, near the railway tracks. The walls were made of brick, without plaster on them, and the roof had asbestos sheets. Every year, the monsoons brought along its set of problems, including leakages from the roof. Subhash was not bothered about tending to such problems, and it would be left to Ramesh to cover the roof with a plastic sheet. He would usually look for used flex sheets at the sales office of the construction site that he was working at, and bring them home.

"Allright, stop crying now. Once papa returns, we will ask him to fix it."

Saee tried to console Seema, as she looked for a bowl. She tried to position it on the bed in a way that it could catch the falling drops. It had been raining incessantly for the last ten days, and somehow the water had managed to find its way down, in-between the flex and the asbestos.

The bed was placed along the wall opposite the brown door to the room and in a corner. On one side of the room, an old wooden table served as a kitchen tabletop. Over this table, a utensil stand was fixed to the wall with nails. Next to the table, Ramesh had managed to fix an old sink, which served as the common washing point for utensils as well as for clothes. A small window over the sink served as a source of ventilation and natural light into the small room.

The Rich Labourer

On the opposite side, a cupboard served as a television stand and a common storage for Seema's books and a few clothes. On the wall next to it, nails were driven into the wall and a few shirts, trousers and frocks hung from them. Next to the television set, the charging end of a mobile charger lay, that Ramesh and Saee used in turns. Electricity was a saving grace with near zero downtime. Ramesh had fixed an oscillating wall fan on the leg-end of the bed. A solitary CFL lamp on the head-side of the bed, served as the only source of light in the room. Seema and Rohit slept on the bed at night while Saee and Ramesh would sleep over a light quilt on the floor. The quilt would be rolled and kept on top of the cupboard in the morning.

The bed served as a place for the kids to work on their books and drawings. It would also serve as a working top for Saee; she would often sit on the bed and chop vegetables, while preparing food.

The house lacked a toilet and the family had to depend on the community toilets that the municipality had set up. Although it was just about thirty metres from their room, there would still be a long queue in the mornings. Ramesh would often use the open ground near the railway tracks to do his thing.

Ramesh had dreams of becoming rich when he left his village, but after so many years in Mumbai he was just another poor labourer in a big bad city. Thankfully he got regular work with a contractor that he had now worked

The Rich Labourer

with for five years. However given the sluggish pace of the industry there would be a few weeks during the year, when he would have no work. With two growing kids, life was tough and the family struggled to make ends meet. Ramesh did not have a bank account. In between his and Saee's income, they would keep aside small amounts in an old tin box, as and when they could. They felt that this would come handy for the kids' studies.

"Maa, I am hungry." Seema uttered as her tears dried up.

"That's good, get your plate. I have made your favourite alu sabji today." Saee sounded relieved. Rohit had woken up with all the crying by now. Seema quickly served both of them with the potato curry and rotis, which they relished. She too grabbed her plate and quickly had her lunch. It was nearly two in the afternoon, and she was getting late to go to Riya's apartment, to do the dishes. She worked as a maid with two families and made two trips; once in the morning and then in the afternoon. In the mornings, the kids would be with Ramesh, who would drop them at the municipal school located on the main road abutting the slums. The two of them would walk back home, along with other kids from their neighbourhood, by around noon. In her second shift, Saee would usually make the kids sleep and do the rounds.

"Allright now, time to sleep." Saee hurried Seema and Rohit to bed as she quickly washed the plates. She felt safe leaving them alone for the ninety minutes or so, mainly

The Rich Labourer

because of the presence of the neighbours on the ground level of their room. They were a kind family, from the same village near Pune, and while Padmini worked as a maid, her mother in law, Purala stayed at home and looked after Padmini's two young sons. Purala also kept an eye on Rohit and Seema in the afternoons.

"OK bye Mausi" Saee waved to Purala as she caught a glance of her through a small window while walking down the steps.

"Don't worry, walk slowly." said Purala, as she cautioned Saee about the slippery pathways inside the slums. The pathways were laid with granite stones; although individual families kept them quite clean, they would be slippery due to the rains. She hurried towards the main exit from the slums onto the main road.

As she stepped on to the main road and took a right turn towards Riya's apartment blocks at Sunrise Apartments, Saee suddenly felt the ground empty below her feet. She slipped on something slimy and fell down with a thud on the ground. Although shocked, she managed to quickly get back on her feet. No damage appeared to have been done, although her saree got a bit messed up. A quick survey determined that she had slipped on a banana peel lying on the road, near the garbage bin.

A large metallic municipal garbage bin had been on that spot near the main entry to the slums, for as long as she could remember. It always seemed to be overflowing with garbage, and appeared to be on a low priority for the municipality to clear it regularly.

"Some things never change; Swachh Bharat my foot!", muttered Saee as she rubbed her Saree and a huge poster with a picture of the Prime Minister caught her eye, just across the road.

₹₹₹

Three years back, the new government at the centre had launched the "Swachh Bharat Abhiyan" with much fanfare. Positioned as a mission to clean up India, the then new Prime Minister had announced it, soon after setting up his new government. Symbolic photo ops of the Prime Minister himself cleaning streets with a broom encouraged several publicity hungry celebrities to follow suit. A widespread campaign across electronic and print media followed, urging Indians to keep their surroundings clean. The campaign itself seemed to have been quite successful in raising the awareness level for the need to be clean, across different strata of society. However, nothing much seems to have changed, on the ground in urban areas; as a severe lack of an implementation plan became evident.

The only 'on-ground' activity that Saee remembered around the Swachh Bharat Abhiyan, is a local politician visiting their locality about two years back, taking a broom in his hands and posing for pictures. When the broom was

The Rich Labourer

replaced with a mic the politician went on to say that the garbage bin would be removed from the locality and municipal sweepers would sweep the streets near the slums daily. He then went on to distribute sweets and later won the municipal elections from the locality. On that day, the garbage bin was emptied and the surroundings cleaned. Post his winning the elections, everything went back to the way it was.

₹₹₹

Has the Swachh Bharat Abhiyan been a success? The verdict is not yet out. In rural areas the statistics of toilet construction are impressive, despite the mixed response around the usage of the toilets. In urban areas, the hype and fanfare, which accompanied the policy's announcement, was not matched by a near equivalent amount of action on the ground. The human brain works in a manner that if expectations are raised very high, even the slightest hint of results not reflecting such high expectations are read as abject failures by it. So the adage "under-promise, and over-deliver" may come handy while making such lofty promises; the promise of an India which will turn spic and span with the sweep of the Prime Minister's broom, almost overnight.

But then, when it comes to politics, the only way appears to be promises and hope; votes are won largely on the basis of promises, and elections are lost largely on the basis of delivery failures.

The Rich Labourer

How can social problems be addressed in such a scenario?

India's urban centres are the face to the world, which houses its most vocal and influential citizens, and at the same time welcomes influential citizens from all over the world. Given the burgeoning urban population in India, it is well understood that the infrastructure required to clean up the cities is a huge challenge. Planning and will power may not be enough to change things; often it is about cultivating new habits. Indians have deep-seated beliefs about cleanliness and waste disposal.

For example, before praying, Indians have the habit of cleaning up. Such cleanliness is usually linked to purity. The place of worship and its immediate surroundings are cleaned up, usually by the one offering prayers. Others are usually not allowed in this act of cleaning up, demonstrating ownership. However, what is not included in this is sense of ownership, is the cleanliness of the nearby surroundings. It is likely that this sense of limited ownership is linked to past times of scarcity and drought in India.

So one sees squeaky-clean interiors of apartments in Indian cities with filthy surroundings. Similarly there are many other facets of Indian urban life, which hide behind several layers of life on the surface. Such layers have developed over years of following habits. Building infrastructure to clean up Indian cities based on what is visible on the surface may not be enough for Swachh Bharat Abhiyan to be successful in India's urban centres. One needs to dig deeper. One needs to probe. And then ponder, and finally prove.

The 3-P method

The three Ps are Probe-Ponder-Prove. This is a tried and tested method, which can be used to solve any big and small problem. The basis of the method lies in the fact that before we jump to the solution of any problem that we are faced with, we need to spend time probing to define the correct problem, and then synthesizing the insights from such definition, to arrive at a solution. More importantly, this method puts the end user at the centre of the process. It is about human centricity.

During the initial years, the Swachh Bharat Abhiyan appeared to be having a far greater impact in the rural areas, compared to urban areas. It also needs to be understood that the meaning and perception of 'development' is very different for rural folk, as compared to the perception of those living in urban centres. Did the Swachh Bharat Abhiyan centre its solution around Saee's day to day life? Or around Riya's life? If it were, one would have seen some visible changes across India's urban centres. If changes were not seen after three-four years, then who was it designed around?

The Rich Labourer

Probe First

The first thing to do really is to probe well enough to clearly define the problem. Often it is seen that one spends considerable time and effort in the solution of the wrong problem defined. In all the imagery, which comes to one's mind regarding the Swachh Bharat Abhiyan, the top of the mind recall is someone cleaning streets with a broom. That imagery sends out two clear and very strong messages; do not litter streets, and if streets are littered, please clean them up. Was street cleanliness the problem? If it were, it would have been the simplest problem to fix. Just increase the number of sweepers and the frequency of cleaning.

It is of paramount importance, to try and understand what the real problem is, at the user level. If one went out with the traditional tools and started asking Saee, what her problems were, she would not be able to articulate the real problems. Human beings cannot clearly articulate their unmet needs. This is what Steve Jobs meant when he said that he never did market survey before the launch of a product. Humans cannot give one enough feedback about a need which has not been met. So asking alone does not help. Observation needs to be done as well. One needs to observe Saee as she goes through her day-to-day life to try and understand what cleanliness means to her. In a slightly different context what does cleanliness mean to Riya, who lives in an apartment. Is cleanliness about aesthetics or is it

The Rich Labourer

about health and hygiene? Are there some strong habits around these, which need realignment?

During the probe stage, one aims to define the problem correctly. The need to probe comes from the human tendency to be myopic and the inability to look beyond what is visible on the surface.

Then Ponder

Observation to understand the human behind users and their habits leads to hundreds of pages of data. When videography tools are used, one is often left with hours and hours of footage. Such data needs to be synthesized with an aim to identify the correct problem. Once the real problems are identified, ideas to address them will emerge. For example, it may be observed that some people litter streets freely, without thinking much. The insight from this observation is that, people neither value waste nor is there any fear of littering outside of one's home. One can address this by making people realize that waste has value, and one can generate income by processing waste. Secondly, the possibility of penalties for littering streets would further buttress the problem of littering.

Data synthesis gives rise to insights, which leads to solutions. Brain-writing sessions, as well as controlled brainstorming sessions at this stage, helps. It is important to set rules for such sessions, as otherwise it could end without achieving the goals. A "boss is always right" mentality, which leads to group thinking, often acts as an impediment, with a vociferous leader overshadowing multiple ideas. The key is to generate multiple ideas.

It is good to have multiple ideas at this stage; but it is important to quickly pick ones, which are most likely to work. A combination of convergent and divergent thinking is important. In convergent thinking, the group aims towards finding one or two ideas to work upon; whereas in divergent thinking the idea is to have multiple ideas to choose from.

Quickly done rough prototypes of shortlisted ideas is a good method to verify what works and what does not. Rough prototypes go a long way in the iterative process to fine-tune the final solution. Prototyping is not always about making physical models; in case of intangible services, methods like role-playing are effective in determining what may work and what may not.

Finally Prove

A massive nation-wide initiative like Swachh Bharat Abhiyan is likely to elicit multiple solutions. One of the possible solutions, built upon the idea of making people realize the value of waste, could be the setting up of businesses to collect waste and e-waste, and recycle or up-cycle these products or convert waste to energy. Before embarking on the path towards the commercialization of solutions, it is important to do live prototypes and even

The Rich Labourer

pilots if necessary. Whereas it is easy to prototype tangible products, it is equally important to prototype the intangible. This can be easily done through role-plays and soft rollouts of services within a closed group, to gauge the performance.

A pilot, which is a live prototype, run within the contextual eco-system, can help fix any unseen problem, before a commercial launch. A pilot tests the entire system and is not limited to the product or service alone.

The general tendency in problem solving, be it a cleanliness drive or a high-tech product, is to jump to this stage of problem solving, without understanding or defining the problem clearly in the first place. It is important to overcome the psychological inertia to resist change that many in positions of power suffer from. The comfort arising from a leadership position can lead to a position where innovation only means 'incremental improvements' over past glory. Making differently or doing differently allow governments, organisations and people to prove it, by building on the work done during the Probe and Ponder stages.

₹₹₹

"Oh you are late today….", Riya's mother-in-law Keerat Gupta said, as she opened the door for Saee, after hearing the door bell ring.

"Are you OK, what happened?" Keerat asked again, before Saee could reply, noticing her slightly messed up saree and disheveled hair.

"I am OK Maaji…I fell down on the road. Someone had thrown a banana peel on the road and I slipped."

"Oh my God, I hope you have not hurt yourself"

"No Maaji, I am OK." said Saee as she headed towards the kitchen.

Saee did only the dishes at this hour in the Gupta household. Keerat would usually finish her lunch by this hour, and would wait for Saee to come and finish the dishes, before she took her afternoon siesta. She had been following this schedule for the last ten years, ever since she started living with her eldest son Pankaj in Mumbai.

Originally from Chandigarh, Pankaj had started his professional career in Mumbai fifteen years back, after he completed his MBA, with specialization in human resources, from Pune. Pankaj had risen quickly in his career and was now the national director of HR, Facilities & Admin at Paceman, a global agency specializing in running outsourced call centres and BPOs. Pankaj's workplace at Malad was a good forty minutes drive in the mornings from home, and he would usually leave home at nine. He often worked long hours and rarely reached back home before ten in the night.

The Rich Labourer

Riya on the other hand was a chartered accountant, and worked with VM Associates, a top-notch accountancy firm, located at Bandra. While Pankaj kept a driver, Rakesh, she would drive herself. She left around the same time as Pankaj, but would reach back home much earlier, usually by seven in the evening.

The Guptas had two offsprings, Neil and Garima. At twelve, Neil was the elder of the two, while his younger sister was eight. They both went to the same school, Royal High School, and left home together at seven. Travelling by the school bus, they would be back by half past three, allowing Keerat just enough time for a ninety minutes siesta.

"Please send him up" Saee whispered into the intercom mouthpiece as she answered the call from the apartment block's security officer at the ground floor. He had called to inform that the postman had some letters to deliver. Saee tried to keep the noise level down as Keerat had dozed off by now. She went back to the living room, opened the main door and waited there for the postman to arrive, lest he should ring the door bell and wake up Keerat.

Pankaj and Riya had purchased this three-bedroom apartment nine years back when the property prices had dipped. The seventeen storey tower at Andheri West, was located close to the suburban railway network, and was part of a three building complex that the developer Prathamesh Builders had developed over five years. It had turned out to be a good buy and the buildings were well maintained, and looked as good as new, even after nine years.

In recent years, Pankaj and Riya had begun to feel the tiredness of the day-to-day commute to and from work and the increasing workload. Both of them loved the work they did, but often felt overwhelmed by the seemingly unending running around for one thing or the other that the city demanded. With the traffic getting worse every year and activities around the kids academics increasing, things were not getting any easier. They also felt that the kids ought to be exposed to a different, free-er way of living, where open spaces and open minds ruled. Pankaj had spent his early years in the wide expanse of Chandigarh, whereas Riya had spent her childhood in a large house in a green neighbourhood of Pune. The two would often discuss the possibility of quitting the corporate rat race and shifting to Pune.

Pankaj would travel often to Pune as Paceman had a large centre in the city, besides other centres in Gurgaon, Hyderabad and in Bangalore. As the business was growing Pankaj was always under pressure, especially with the recruitments, as well as with the facilities expansion. He was paid well, but he often felt suffocated in the midst of his high-pressure work life, which left him with little time to even think of anything else.

The Rich Labourer

"Ding dong! Ding dong!" the doorbell rang as Keerat recognized the standard practice of Neil ringing it twice.

"Coming, coming, beta." Keerat said out loud as she approached the door.

2

Defining the problem

Two years back, Riya's boss Vinod had entrusted her with the responsibility of driving a Corporate Social Responsibility ("CSR") project. Vinod, in his early fifties, had amassed good wealth through his flourishing practice; but he was not one who liked to keep it all for himself. He paid his staff of thirty well; and at the same time he always felt the need to 'give back' to society.

Riya's responsibility was to identify a good social cause that they could get involved in and then stay with the cause till it was ready to effect measurable impact. Riya, helped by

The Rich Labourer

two energetic juniors, Mohan and Priya, had spent a good three months evaluating various causes. At the end of many hours of study, brainstorming and late nights, the team of three had decided to pick up the cause of providing solar power to rural communities which were not connected to the grid. Riya realized that many rural communities also lived in houses which were poorly built, leaked during the monsoons, was very hot in the summers and very cold in the winters. Moreover solar power had always been seen as an 'after-thought' even in urban and semi-urban communities; it had never been integrated with the design of the house. Riya wanted to consider marrying the two. What if they could develop a reasonably priced, good quality house where solar power generation and storage capabilities were integrated?

Such a solution may not only address the power issue, but also address many of the problems arising out of living in poorly built homes.

Lack of electricity is a barrier to overcoming poverty. Without electricity, people are at a disadvantage in nearly every aspect of their lives. Having electricity means the ability to study at night and get an education. It means the difference between subsistence farming and backbreaking labour, and having the technology to create large enough crop yields to make a living. It allows people to have and power cell phones, which are being used across the

The Rich Labourer

developing world for mobile banking and to access the Internet.

On the other hand, living in poorly built homes, which lack good insulation and ventilation, often make inhabitants sick. Falling sick is not only debilitating but also eats up into income which could otherwise be spent on education.

Having access to electricity and living in a good quality solid home would empower such people, in more ways than one, socially and economically. Riya and team decided to name the project Powerhouse.

Riya knew that they would be able to prove their hypothesis if they went beyond a research report and link theory to practice. For this they would need to get their hands dirty. The Powerhouse team decided to use the 3-P method to address the issue. Instead of jumping onto Internet based research, they decided to clearly define the physical context. For this, the team zeroed down on a remote village called Rampur outside Nasik. It was still off-grid, although the local political leaders had promised to get electricity within the next two years. The villagers burnt kerosene lamps, a few would run diesel generators for business and most people would walk miles to charge their mobile phones.

Probe

At the core of the probe stage is the acceptance of the fact that users cannot clearly articulate what they want. Team Powerhouse employed the services of a bunch of ten final year students of Architecture to do some research in Rampur.

Secondary Research: Riya divided the bunch of students and put the first team on the job to conduct focused secondary research on the solar power market in India, specific to households. The team began to explore the most recent news in the field and extensively used the Internet, newspapers, magazines and trade journals that they could lay their hands upon. They looked up recent innovations in solar power technology and studied which of the breakthroughs had worked and which had not. Given that policies were fast changing in this space in India, they read up about the incentives given by various governments to promote solar and other renewable sources of power.

Expert Opinion: Team two were given the task of speaking with industry experts and take their feedback on the topic at hand. They began by first determining the kind of experts they needed to speak with and came down to a list of policy interventionists, academicians, solar power component manufacturers, NGOs and energy consultants.

Then they went about conducting structured interviews with such professionals and received systems-level views

The Rich Labourer

on the topic, heard about recent innovations—successes and failures—and also got the perspectives of organizations like banks, governments and NGOs.

Life Beyond Data: A third team was assigned the responsibility of collecting primary data through a structured questionnaire. The students visited Rampur and two other, similar villages and spoke to the villagers. While conventional methods of primary and secondary data collection helped in getting hard data on the table; Riya soon realized that questionnaire based studies were not helping in understanding the real unmet needs of the locals. She wanted to understand the lives of people at a human level, behind the layers of data.

For one week, Riya pitched camp in the village along with Priya and Mohan. The family of the village headman, Sukhatme, hosted them. Sukhatme had the largest house in the village with four rooms; it had plastered brick walls and a tiled roof. In this house lived Sukhatme and his wife and their two sons, with their respective wives and three grandchildren. Riya, Priya and Mohan were given two rooms to share amongst themselves. Sukhatme had a diesel generator that he used for about three hours every evening; the village folk would go to sleep by nine and most would start their day by five in the morning.

Rampur, with thirty homes, was located about a kilometer from Jategaon. Jategaon was a much larger congregation with about one hundred homes. It was just off the Nasik-

The Rich Labourer

Mumbai highway, and hence had easy access to the outside world, including a petrol pump on the highway. Amongst other benefits, Jategaon enjoyed grid based electric supply, although the supply was erratic. Jategaon was also famous for its Sunday bazaar, where folks from smaller nearby hamlets would flock once a week to buy and sell goods. It also had a primary school. The villagers from Rampur depended on Jategaon for their diesel as well as other non-essential goods like construction materials.

Riya and her team spent the daytime observing the people of Rampur; and even went inside their homes to see and feel how they lived, day-to-day. They conducted structured interviews, but Riya saw value in digging beyond the structure, getting friendly with the villagers and learning about facets not covered under the structure. They ate with the villagers inside their homes. On one night they stayed with a family who did not have a generator and depended on kerosene lamps for light. Many hours of conversations took place during such times; and some of these conversations were casual, unstructured ones, in an effort to understand the ethos behind actions that people took. The team used videography and digital voice recorders to record some of these conversations.

All of this gave a good understanding about the lives of the villagers to the Powerhouse team. However the team wanted to take things one-step forward. They wanted to understand what electricity really meant for the villagers.

The Rich Labourer

Was it only about light? Or about running a fan during the hot months? Or was it much more?

When questions were asked from a structured format, the villagers could not articulate clearly what they really wanted from the supply of electricity, as most of them had never experienced the luxury of living in houses which got regular electricity. They could not define what they had not experienced.

This is important to understand. People cannot clearly express what they want from a product or a service, if they have not seen or experienced it.

Henry Ford famously said when horse drawn carriages still ruled, "If I asked my customers what they wanted, they would have probably said – A faster horse."

A Collage: There are various non-traditional methods to get to know what end-users really want. One of the methods is to use collages. Riya decided to use the collage method on the villagers. One morning, before the sun was too high in the sky, Riya and team, got together a large number of villagers under the large banyan tree near Sukhatme's house.

Sukhatme had made arrangements for the thirty odd mix of male and female villagers who had gathered, to sit on the shade below the large tree. Mats were laid on the ground and arrangements for drinking water were made. For nearly three hours, team Powerhouse and the villagers got involved in an exercise which was insightful, yet a lot of fun.

Riya and team asked the thirty participants to show them what having electricity in their homes meant to them. Amidst a mixture of skepticism, smiles and laughter, the group of thirty was divided into five groups. Each group was provided with images, relevant words on small chits, and magazines. They were told to create a collage with these, depicting what electricity meant to them. For this, they were given large A1 sheets of white paper, gum, sketch-pens and scissors; and asked to stick cut-outs on it of what they felt reflected their idea of having electricity. They could cut images from the magazines, or make some drawing, or stick some of the words given to them, or write their own words or combine all of it. Riya helped by showing the villagers a couple of examples of what the final sheet could look like.

In the beginning, Riya's team assumed that the villagers would come up with images of a lit up home, of a child studying, etc.—images that spoke of the importance of light in their homes. After all, the generic name used for electricity has been 'light' for most people in India. What surprised them, however, was that light was far more nuanced in the minds of the villagers. People were drawn to images of televisions, mobile phones, families, and community events.

When the team asked people to explain why they chose these images, they said that electricity could go far beyond the ability to have a light bulb in their homes. Being able to watch television and being updated with what was happening in the world scored far higher than a light bulb in their minds. A primary need expressed was the ability to charge mobile phones at home. It was also becoming clearer that most villagers felt that the community could prosper socio-economically as a whole if electricity allowed them to do some things together.

This exercise gave powerful insights to team Powerhouse. Coupled with the experience of living with the community for a week, the team came back to Mumbai, armed with some very powerful data.

The Probe phase is about learning on the fly, opening oneself up to creative possibilities, and trusting that as long as one remains grounded in desires of the communities one is engaging with, ideas will evolve into the right solutions. One builds the team, gets smart on the challenge, and talks to a staggering variety of people.

Ponder

During this phase, one shares what one has learned with the team, make sense of a vast amount of data, and identify opportunities for design. Lots of ideas are generated, many of which are thrown in the waste paper bin and some are kept. Tangibility begins to appear, as rough prototypes of ideas are built, then by sharing them with the people from whom one has learned, one gets their feedback. Iterations and refinement follows, until it is felt that the solution is ready for the world.

So far Riya was working with Priya and Mohan. Upon her return from Rampur she realized that it was about time, in the project's life cycle, when a cross-disciplinary team was put together. From the experts who were interviewed, Riya got three more members on board. Ravi the Architect, Sukanya the Electrical Engineer and Kishan the solar expert. It was well understood that the team would have to work with a much larger network of professionals over time as they went along, given the 'socio-economic' nature of the project. Given the noble nature of the project, all three had agreed to work on the project on a pro-bono basis, with a revenue share agreement once the solution was commercialized.

The Powerhouse team began to meet on Saturdays. They would use the large Yoga room at VM Associates. It was a room with a high ceiling; large windows on one side, a white board and projection facility on one side and the other two walls had fabric paneling. They would have the Yoga mats rolled up in the corner and got some beanbags in. They primarily worked on the floor and on the walls.

The Rich Labourer

Sharing Information: The process started with each member sharing the information gathered. Walls were filled with post-its pasted on A1 sheets of paper that each member used, to communicate their learnings. They supported these with story telling and imagery on the overhead projection system. These sheets were stuck on the fabric panels and the team went over them, around the room, one by one.

These downloading sessions were not one-way and involved questions from the listeners. At times, these would turn into what is traditionally understood as brainstorming sessions. However there is always a risk of such sessions ending up open-ended with no solutions in sight. Recognising this, Riya loosely controlled these sessions, practicing and encouraging a mix of divergent and convergent thinking. For some time, in a divergent mode, she would welcome the wildest of ideas. As more and more ideas would pour in; she would get the group to converge on a few. The group would then further go divergent on the shortlisted few and then converge again. They would do this multiple times till a broad consensus was arrived at.

Observations to Insights: During the team's stay for a week in the village, they had noticed that some of the men, at night, would take out the *khatia* at night and sleep on it outside their homes. On further investigation they learnt that villagers, during the hot summer months, would do

The Rich Labourer

this, as the insides of the poorly made brick houses would get very hot in the night. Without a fan, sleeping in the open air, especially under a tree, with a soothing natural breeze, was more comfortable than sleeping inside. During these hot months, the womenfolk and children would have sleepless nights as they tossed and turned through the night, trying to get sleep.

Families, during summer nights, wanted a cooler, well ventilated room to sleep in. This was an insight statement.

The Powerhouse team had documented all the observations, in various forms like pictures, videos, notes and voice recordings. Now they began to document the insights in the form of insights statements like these.

When Riya wrote down the insight statement on the board, Kishan asked Ravi:

"So Ravi, how can we provide them with a house, which will be cooler during the summer months, and perhaps warmer during the winter months?"

The team had learned that the poorly insulated homes were bitterly cold inside during the winter months and although this was not part of their direct observation, Kishan's question to Ravi took the insight to a deeper level.

The team soon realised that the observations were leading them to insights and these insights were further egging them on with "How can we" questions; which had the potential to lead them to solutions. Priya took up the task of listing this down, in a table format, with the following column titles:

Observation>Insight>How Can We>Ideas>Solutions

Ideas & Concepts: Ideas now began to flow with ease. With wild ideas being welcomed, this was an exciting time for the team as the team went into play mode with their thinking hats. Along with newer ideas from emerging insights, the team was also encouraged to build on the ideas of others. With this, the team could go on a divergent mode and multiple ideas emerged for each insight.

By now, Riya had become skilled in the art of channelizing this energy by practicing a mix of divergent and convergent thinking. A look at multiple ideas made it clear that some of these could be bundled together, for a potentially much stronger solution than the individual strength of ideas.

Riya introduced the team to brain-writing, as she often found this to be highly effective in idea generation. She would make the team of five write down 3 ideas on a worksheet within five minutes. At the end of five minutes the sheet would be passed on to the next team member on the right. The process would be repeated and each member would be free to get inspired from the idea he or she read on the sheet written by his or her neighbour and contribute to them by integrating or completing them, or decide to ignore them and start a new one from scratch. The process goes on until the worksheet is completely filled, and the team would generate over seventy ideas in thirty minutes this way.

Ideation is multi layered and at every layer the team faced the challenge of accepting a few and rejecting many. At every layer and at the end of every session, Riya made it a habit of spending the last few minutes to arrive at a team consensus on shortlisting five top ideas. The team would then move on to the next stage only with these five ideas. This helped the team to stay broadly focused during a stage where the multiplication of ideas made it difficult to remain so.

The team, in the journey from insights to ideas, juxtaposed them against the research done earlier and the experts' insights and opinions. This helped them filter at every stage, as ideas went through an unstructured, yet effective, feasibility test. Slowly a few broad concepts began to appear; some of which became stronger with time and some weaker. Rough concepts looked somewhat like:

- A sustainable house
- An off-site manufactured house
- A house which would generate its own power
- A house which would allow a family to spend quality time together
- A house which would effect economic freedom

The Rich Labourer

Emerging concepts were much fewer in number, as compared to ideas. With these written down, the team was closer to solutions now. Like ideas, Riya now began to encourage the team to bundle together concepts. So a bundling of the above would look something like:

"An off-site manufactured sustainable home, which uplifts rural families socio-economically."

By indicating that the house would uplift a rural family socio-economically, this was going one step forward, by clearly setting out the desired end result. This approach was repeated across concepts; and helped the team not only to work on solutions but also to keep the desired end result in mind. In social innovation, a solution on the drawing board, without impacting lives on the ground, is meaningless.

The Rich Labourer

3

Mapping the journey

Developing empathy through Role Play

Riya's father was a theatre actor and as a child she spent her days at home in the midst of dramatics. He took voluntary retirement from his job at a centralized bank at the peak of his career, to follow his passion and became a full time stage actor at forty-five. Fellow actors would drop by at their large home in Pune every other day. A large empty room was dedicated for practice sessions, and she would often sit around, especially during her holidays, quietly absorbing all the theatrics. Once in a while, she would play bit roles in some of the plays; her father taking care to ensure that there was no compromise with academics. During her graduation, she was an active member of the college theatre club. Although she had half a mind to pursue it as a career, she eventually decided otherwise. Riya did not give up dramatics completely and dabbled at it as a hobby, often helping kids from her residential complex during social events.

Early immersion into drama had greatly benefited Riya as a person in her journey of life. Not only had it given her enormous self-confidence, she had also developed good communication skills, besides developing an ability to concentrate under most situations. Understanding characters, roles and the subtext of plays had allowed her to relate better to different situations, backgrounds, and cultures. Riya often felt that she was able to show compassion and tolerance for others, and developed a sense of empathy, because of her days spent in dramatics. It was empathy at work when Riya spent those days in the village, living and eating with families. It was empathy at work, which allowed Riya to be comfortable doing corporate presentations at five star hotels.

At team Powerhouse, Riya used the power of dramatics to test some of the ideas; to get into character and act it out such that they could experience it. By role-playing, she was doing fast prototypes of the various experiences that end users could potentially have.

The Rich Labourer

She would pick up some of the shortlisted ideas and get the team members to enact various roles like a skit and play it out. All of this was within the four walls of the Yoga room and the team learnt much; way before they got the ideas out of the office confines. She would take some time to identify the necessary roles, who would play them, and what was it that they would be looking to test—is it the effectiveness of a sales pitch or a interaction that an end user would have within Powerhouse, how would an end user respond to the product? Given her dramatics background, she could quickly conjure up costumes and props, which were highly effective tools in bringing role-play to life.

By now, the team had begun to appreciate the importance of empathy; that special skill which allows you to put yourself in the shoes of others. They were now at a stage where they were trying to figure out things from the end-user's standpoint; how they would experience Powerhouse.

Although Powerhouse was conceived as a tangible product, Riya well understood that the services component of it would be high. Given that it was a self powered home with integrated generation and storage capabilities, it required a 'service approach' to keep the house performing at high efficiency levels for twenty five years or more. All solar panel manufacturers were working on a twenty-five years warranty basis; so the challenge was to keep the house running and performing optimally for at least twenty-five years. The team had to adopt the thinking and philosophy of designing a high tech product like a car or a refrigerator. It was being conceived as the first house, which would have a user manual. Users would be guided on how to run the house; they would also get continuous updates on any upgrades and any possible improvements to Powerhouse.

Powerhouse was also expected to uplift families and communities at a socio-economic level. It would be a solid and a hygienic house, which would reduce health issues and allow children to study regularly. It would also allow end-users to skill themselves in the erection of houses in the community, allowing them extra income.

All this and many more benefits were being imagined at this ideation stage. What was emerging was that it would be a completely new experience for people. Every aspect during the entire life-cycle of buying and living in a Powerhouse would be new. One would be able to buy a house like buying a two wheeler, one would not have to ever worry about power, about light in the nights, one would have to run and maintain it like they would maintain a two wheeler.

Experience Journey Map

Riya encouraged the team to map out the experience for an end user. While role-play helped, she got Rohan to put this down, graphically. Rohan tried to put himself in the shoes of a buyer and put down the milestones in the journey from hearing about Powerhouse, to buying it and living in it for many years.

An experience journey map captures the story of the customer's experience: from first contact, through the process of engagement and into a long-term relationship. It identifies key interactions that the customer has with the selling or servicing organization. It captures user's feelings, motivations and questions for each of these touch points. It often provides a sense of the customer's greater motivation. What do they wish to achieve, and what are their expectations of the product or service?

An experience journey map is laid out graphically and a good way to start is to identify the various touch points that a customer is likely to have with a product or a service. For example, in case of a consumer product like a mobile phone meant for the urban educated youth, the following give an indication of what type of touch points may emerge.

- Marketing Channels (Email, Postal, Telephone, Facebook, Blogs, etc);
- Order Fulfilment (Delivery, Payment, Returns, etc);
- Research Channels (Website, Consumer Forums, Store, Customer Services, etc).

Over and above these direct touch points there may be various indirect ones via social sites, word of mouth, and customer reviews. All of these need to be considered as well, in order to understand how a customer will interact with a brand and co-create value for it. The customer will behave differently for different industries or different products, with the following common traits over a period of time in the journey:

- Awareness
- Discovery
- Purchase
- Use of product or service
- Bonding

Value is created when bonding takes place.

Rohan impressed the group with the infographics that he came up with in his experience journey map. It gave the group a framework that enabled the team to further improve the customer experience that they were trying to develop.

Prototyping, Feedback and Iterations

By now Ravi, Sukanya and Kishan had become active participants in the ideation sessions.

Ravi was rather outspoken and he kept coming up with multiple ideas about the shape and structure of the house, at every stage. The research done earlier by the students of Architecture helped. Ravi, besides his practice in

The Rich Labourer

Architecture, was a guest lecturer in colleges of Architecture. Unlike many others in his field, he was one who truly believed in the power of student driven research and ideation. He always felt that young minds bring in originality in thinking.

Sukanya, who came from a family of engineers, often said during team meetings;

"I feel I am back in college, this time a co-ed one!"

During her graduation in electrical engineering at IIT Kharagpur, she was one of three girls in a batch of sixty. While one of the other girls became a banker, the other took to teaching and Sukanya remained the only lady from her batch to continue to do pure engineering. After ten years of working in a large engineering consultancy, she had recently started off on her own. The freedom of being an entrepreneur allowed her flexibility to dabble in things that she enjoyed. Conventionally, electrical engineers join teams, once the basic design of the structure or the product is at an advanced stage. However, at team Powerhouse, Sukanya was involved from its inception and never missed a meeting; it was important for all team members to be fully involved and co-create solutions. Team Powerhouse wanted to leverage the power of cross-disciplinary contributions to the solution.

Kishan often pulled Sukanya's leg by saying she was one of the boys in the team. The team had developed a good

The Rich Labourer

rapport within themselves by now. Yet Riya had cultivated a strict disciplinary culture during the working sessions. Once in a while, post a tiring session, the team would go out together for a coffee or a drink. Kishan took the lead in this.

Kishan was the happy go lucky 'rich parents' son' who had taken serious interest in solar energy during the last five years. His father was a moneyed businessman from Surat, with interests in trading, housing and the stock markets. Kishan was 'sent' to study mechanical engineering at Oxford University, UK. Post his graduation, he got a chance to work with a large Photo Voltaic ("PV") manufacturer in Frankfurt, Germany. With just about one hundred sunny days, Germany had remained the top global solar energy producer for years. India with three hundred sunny days, lagged behind. Kishan quickly realized the huge potential for the growth and development of the sector in India. After two years in Germany, he came back to India and took up a job as principal designer with Solarz One in Ahmedabad, which was one of the largest manufacturers of solar panels in India. His father encouraged him on this move as he realized that one day Kishan may be able to help him set up solar farms in Gujarat. The new solar policy from the government did make it sound like a very profitable sector.

Kishan had left his job at Solarz One to join the Powerhouse team and shifted to Mumbai. When he was

The Rich Labourer

not spending time on Powerhouse, he would spend time on researching on the latest developments in the industry. He would also visit exhibitions and conferences across the world to keep himself and the team updated . Unmarried at thirty-two, Kishan, carried the additional reputation of being a party animal on weekends. Of jovial nature, he was a team player, and kept the team in high spirits at all times.

In their early thirties, what helped was that Sukanya, Ravi and Kishan were from the same age group. There was great chemistry between the three, and the rest of the team as well. Sukanya and Kishan contributed whole-heartedly to Ravi's ideas on how the structure should look.

By now, Powerhouse had begun to take tangible shape as Ravi helped shape a house that would be modular, not only in its process of erection, but also structurally. The foundation of the house would be the only major 'on-site' construction in the house; most of the other components in the house would be factory manufactured and erected on site, like a car is assembled in a factory. While a family of two could buy a small 240 sqft unit, the same family could also add rooms, over time, as the family size increased.

Ravi regularly showed his concept in the form of sketches to the team so that everyone could visualize. He drew hand sketches and also took the help of tools like Google SketchUp for fast visualization. Sometimes he would also use cardboard and thermocol to make rough models of the house. The team was now beginning to experience rapid prototyping.

Rapid Prototyping or Fast Prototyping puts an idea to test before it comes face to face with the market. Such rough prototypes not only save time, but often help to focus on critical elements. One could learn something like "Which part of the roof should the solar panel be fitted on?" or "Should the roof be flat or sloping?" Hundreds of questions surround a team at the Ponder stage and rapid prototyping is a great way to answer them. Some of the key benefits include:

1. Tangibility: Rapid prototyping gives tangible shape to concepts and helps the team to carry forward their ideas and implement them in their design prior to finalization.

2. Immediate Iteration: It becomes easy to iterate and incorporate changes quickly, especially with feedback from end-users. With each iteration, the design improves further, building confidence for both the team as well as the end user.

3. Saving Cost and Time: Making a complete working prototype involves substantial time and cost with the need to develop moulds, patterns, CNC machines and special tools. With sketches and rough cardboard models, rapid prototyping helps save a lot of time and money.

4. Mass Customization : Although standardization is the key for high efficiency, mass customization is the order of the day with products and services being standardized for certain regions. So even a product like Powerhouse would need to be mass customized for various geographic regions due to meteorological and cultural differences. Rapid prototyping allows such mass customization to be experimented with, at an early stage and requires no special tools or processes to implement design changes in the product.

5. Minimizing Design Flaws: The ability to visualize a tangible product allows the team to identify flaws in the design, prior to mass production. The risks of faults and usability issues can be identified earlier to avoid problems that might occur later.

The technical team of Ravi-Sukanya-Kishan gained much from playing around with cardboard and thermocol models. Supplemented by sketches and computer animated imagery, the team could visualize the various tangible possibilities of Powerhouse. Feedback and suggestions came in abundance and in quick frequency and this allowed continuous improvement in the product.

₹₹₹

"Lets take it to the people now." Riya said one day, after the team had arrived at a general consensus on the look, size and shape of the house.

The Rich Labourer

"Now? When we are yet to finalise so many things?" Ravi was puzzled.

"Now is the perfect time." Riya insisted.

Riya knew what she was doing. Although everything was not finalized, there was much to gain from giving the end-users a glimpse of the future. It was important at this stage to understand the end-user's perspective. There were two slightly varying designs, which had emerged, and Riya wanted to understand which of the two was the preferred choice. She knew that the exercise would give them other critical feedback, besides helping choose between A and B.

The students of Architecture were called in once again. They were divided into two teams of three each and each team was asked to make a different physical model of Powerhouse. They were given a week for this; which was sufficient for them, given the simplistic nature of the house.

In a week's time, Riya, Priya and Ravi made an early morning start to Rampur with two models and large printouts with graphics depicting various facets of Powerhouse. They had informed Sukhatme, the headman, in advance and he had made arrangements for a gathering of about twenty-five people, under the banyan tree near his house. News of the Powerhouse team's visit had spread and although twenty people were informed, nearly double that number turned up.

The Rich Labourer

The two models were laid out, side by side, on two tables with enough distance between them for people to move around. The prints on A1 sheets of paper were anchored to a quickly arranged cloth-lines, tied to the banyan tree at one end and a smaller tree at the other end.

Riya first allowed Ravi to take centre-stage. Ravi updated the villagers on what the team had been up to since the last time the Powerhouse team was in Rampur, over three months back. Then he went on to explain the various facets of the concept house with the aid of the print-outs and the two models. Then Riya took over. In a structured and carefully orchestrated session, she solicited the feedback from the villagers on specific aspects, through a series of exercises.

It is always important to keep the people one is designing for, at the centre of the project and getting feedback on ideas and prototypes allows one to do that. It also keeps the innovation team on the path of designing something that would be embraced by the end-users. Even if a part of the ideation is rejected, one should not be discouraged; it only shows what will not work, and that's a huge learning. Getting feedback from end-users pushes things forward, and in the right direction.

For maintaining human centricity, it is crucial to integrate end-user feedback into the development of the product or service. One could continue to iterate multiple times, based on such feedback and keep on taking back the prototypes

The Rich Labourer

to the end-users for feedback. This allows continuous refinement of ideas until it becomes something, which will be easily embraced.

This is what Riya and her team did. Over the next five months they had many more brainstorming and brainwriting sessions. They revisited the experience journey map again and again; spoke to experts, built more models, in an effort to tie up all loose ends. They made progress on other aspects of the design process as they started brainstorming on logos and branding aspects as well. They went back once more to the village for further feedback and by inserting the villagers directly into the design process itself, the team came to absorb much more than they could have from mere interviews. They learned about social dynamics in Rampur, how education and healthcare meant so much to them and how an initiative, which gave women dignity, might have a chance at sustainability.

Team Powerhouse was now beginning to have a clear vision of how the project should work, how Powerhouse should communicate and how financial viability would work. Ravi had gone beyond the concept stage and had prepared drawings for construction of a prototype. He had also taken the help of a structural consultant to get the structural drawings ready. The superstructure would be made of concrete panels and with help from the students of Architecture, he had shortlisted three pre-casters for this. Similarly Sukanya had done the electrical design and

The Rich Labourer

Kishan had designed the solar panels. Ravi did a good job of integrating the solar panels into the design in a manner that they looked very much a part of the design and enhanced the look of Powerhouse. The design provided for power storage such that lights could be turned on at night and batteries were required for that. Ravi had worked out a niche in the design of the house specifically meant for the batteries, where they neatly fitted in, without coming in the way of anything.

Every minute detail was thought through. In the final design, nothing looked out of place. Team Powerhouse was very happy with the final outcome. After nearly six months post the first feedback from the villagers on the prototype, they were ready with the design of the house, the business process, brand identity and was now ready to prove that it works.

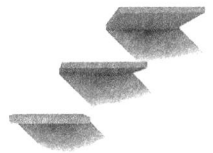

The Rich Labourer

The Rich Labourer

Doing it

Prove

"Lets build it at Badlapur" Vinod reacted at the end of a presentation from the team.

Vinod was mighty impressed with the meticulous detailing in the project. The team was now suggesting that they needed to build a live prototype and Vinod offered his plot of land for the same. He had invested in a plot of land at Badlapur, near Mumbai, a few years back, in the hope of building a country home some day. He had never managed to find the time to explore that; so it had turned out to be a camping spot for his family and friends and occasionally for small groups from the workplace.

"When can we start? How long will it take? Will we be able to live in it?" Vinod could not stop the questions from coming out, in his excitement.

Live prototyping & Piloting

So far all the rapid prototyping done on the project was helpful in communicating the idea to different people. A live prototype would be able to test Powerhouse under real world conditions and prove whether it works or does not. Such a prototype goes a long way in proving the technical feasibility and the business viability of a solution. But Riya wanted to go one step further and wanted to test the desirability as well. She wanted to find out if the villagers of Rampur would accept it or not.

"Vinod, we could start building a live prototype in about six to eight weeks. However I was thinking about building it in Rampur. We could ask a few families to live in the house in turns and get their reactions." Riya responded to Ravi.

"Whoa…slow down Riya."

Riya looked puzzled.

"You guys have done brilliant so far; something very brave and yet noble. Lets get this right. While taking the house to

Rampur is a good idea, I would say that we test it out internally before we take it to people. This will allow us to fix any problems, should they arise, before we take it to them."

Vinod was an astute businessman and well understood the fallacy of taking a new product or service to the market before testing it internally. He had spent enough years managing his own company to understand that anything could go wrong, and often that would come from completely unexpected areas.

"But…." Ravi trailed off.

"Guys, I suggest that we try a live prototype first in Badlapur. Let us be 100% sure that it is technically feasible. It will also give us a sense of the real cost, and will tell us if what looks commercially viable on paper, works in reality as well. Once we have built the house successfully, some of us could spend some time experiencing how it works during the day and during the night. I could even ask Ramu, the caretaker there, to live in the house for a few days. That way we will get all the feedback and be absolutely sure that everything works before we allow the Rampur folk to try it out." Vinod suggested.

It was now making sense to Riya. She added:

"Yes, I think that makes sense. Although we are pretty sure that we have taken care of everything, should any aspect of

The Rich Labourer

the house or the panels require minor modifications, we can still do it, before piloting it in Rampur"

"A pilot…yes that's the word I was looking for. Lets do this live prototype before we pilot it in Rampur" said Vinod.

He also realized that piloting a project like this on the ground and then commercializing it is a totally different ballgame. To do that and to make it a sustainable business the project would call for a much larger team and resources. He was well aware that they were not well equipped with that and perhaps they should allow Powerhouse to be driven by a specialized team beyond the live prototyping stage. After all, they were chartered accountants, and not homebuilders. Perhaps they could partner with someone from the social sector, or someone from the construction sector. Although Vinod was very clear on 'giving back', he knew their limitations and wanted to restrict his team's contribution to finding a solution. Beyond that, he hoped that the solution would be a self-sustaining one.

A Pilot is a sustained engagement with actual end-users, limited to a certain time span or geography. Pilots allow the product to be exposed to all possible market forces; it is no more testing of an idea but testing of the entire system. A pilot allows the team to know if the solution works in the way that it was imagined to work.

The Rich Labourer

Team Powerhouse finally decided to get the live prototype done at Badlapur and look at piloting it at Rampur in the future, after all the kinks, if any, were worked out. They also realized that the live prototype would give them an opportunity to showcase the solution to potential partners and investors.

Way forward

Now that the team had decided to focus on the live prototype, they began to deliberate on the roadmap, up to the live prototype stage and beyond that. Riya soon realized that it would require substantial resources, funding, logistical planning, permits and a whole lot of co-ordination to take Powerhouse beyond the live prototyping stage. She also realized that this appeared complex to them as it was rather specialized, and they would perhaps be better off if they could have a roadmap in a way that the business would be handled by specialists and be self sustainable.

She began to engage the team on roadmap discussions with the focus on:

- Resources
- Funding
- Sustainability

While she took a lead and focused on the broad framework of the above with a window beyond the live prototype, she allowed Ravi to lead the discussions for the live prototype. She became more of an observer during the meetings for the live prototype, as they were rather technical in nature. She picked up valuable inputs from such discussions that helped her frame the medium and long-term goals of the project, and chart the path forward. As she listened more and more, the pieces of the puzzle began to fall in place; Riya began to understand who would be the key stakeholders for the long-term sustainability of Powerhouse. It was becoming clear to her that they would have to address peripheral yet critical issues like access to easy finance for the end-users.

"This is going to be a long haul" she heard herself saying, as she did the mental maths of the timelines associated with milestones in the path towards commercialization of Powerhouse.

Ravi worked out a project schedule for the live prototype with milestones. Riya took a print of a calendar for eighteen months on an A1 sheet of paper, stuck it on one of the walls in the Yoga room and began to put dates on it. She used post-its to write down milestones on the calendar. This allowed for the schedule to be flexible. Different colours of the post-it notes also allowed the team to depict different levels of urgency in milestones. For example, the red ones denoted critical milestones.

Building a Team

Ravi, with ample support from Sukanya and Kishan, began to put together the team required to build the live prototype. As they had already shortlisted potential partners earlier, it did not take them much time to come up with the final list. They quickly got the architectural, structural and other services drawings finalized, prepared Bills of Quantities and secured price quotations through a bidding process. Hard negotiations followed and soon the team was finalized.

"Wow….we saved 15%!"

Ravi announced to the team excitedly, looking at the final cost. On paper, it appeared that they had negotiated a price, which was less by about 15% from the originally estimated number.

"Whats the cost now?" Riya asked.

"Rs. 4,80,000.00, including the panels and the batteries."

"Well, lets not get too excited yet; remember this is a prototype. So we never know." quipped Riya.

Riya was happy at the prospect of offering a solid home with free power under the half million rupees mark. She was hopeful that the price would come down further at the production stage, due to economies of scale. Prototypes always tend to be more expensive than mass produced products. In her mind she began to toy with the idea of these homes being sold like the way vehicles are sold. Perhaps each model of Powerhouse could have two to three versions, like an all basics version, then another model with certain frills, and so on.

She snapped out of it quickly, as she realized that all of this would require them to think beyond their current operational bandwidth. She began to create a framework of all stakeholders who would be required to finally take the project to the market. Vinod was quite clear that once they had the proof of concept, they would like to have the solution handed over to a partner or a consortium that had the adequate skills and resources to pull it off. It was important for the team to put together the broad framework of the team, which would be required for the project to run on its own.

By now Riya had well realized that a multi-disciplinary team was not only necessary but was effective in arriving at novel and often unexpected ideas. For implementation of Powerhouse on a mass scale, they would need specialized know-how, technical capacity, outside partners, and funding.

While building a stakeholders framework, it is important to be clear about how a product or service would be distributed, the capabilities required to do so and the partners needed for that. Once a list of all the capabilities and skills are written down, it becomes easy to identify the type of stakeholders. Some of these may be in-house, and some may be outsourced.

Riya made a stakeholders framework and discussed it with the team. It looked complex at first glance; but made the ecosystem look simple once the inter-connections were understood. Her framework indicated the priority levels of the different capabilities required, and also showed the inter-dependencies between different stakeholders. After three rounds of discussion on the framework, they decided to go with the finalized version, knowing fully well that it might change in the future, depending on the type of partner or partners who would decide to join in the path towards the commercialization of Powerhouse.

Funding Partner

Thankfully the team did not have to worry much about the funding required to build the live prototype. Vinod had allocated a budget of one million Indian rupees for this and Riya was happy that they appeared to be well within that limit. However, in her stakeholders' framework, she had indicated the funder as a high-priority stakeholder.

It is important to have a well thought out funding strategy in place to ensure that a new solution sees the light of the day. It becomes easier to raise money as a project approaches the live prototype stage; however it is prudent to have a funding strategy from the start, rather than depending on the usual buzz generated at the prototype and pilot stage.

There are various ways to raise money. One could apply for grants, or raise money through crowdfunding platforms, or take debt or equity funding. What is important to understand is that each of these paths requires different approaches, slightly different pitches and different relationships to be activated.

Eventually for a product or a service to be self-sustainable, it must pay for everything from the sale of the product. It is important to determine how much money is required to produce the product before this break-even stage is reached. Identify how long it will take to reach this stage.

Depending on the long-term vision for a product or a service and its scalability, additional funds may be required beyond the break-even point, for growth. Growth funding requires a strategy different from the initial funding. A good funding strategy needs to capture the long-term vision as well.

"This is good work, Riya!" Vinod expressed as Riya finished her presentation on the funding strategy.

Vinod had called in two of his trusted senior managers, Jagdish and Nikita for the presentation. Funding is something that they all understood well and Riya was happy that Jagdish and Nikita too liked her ideas. Both volunteered to offer any assistance that Riya might need on finalizing the funding strategy. Riya made minor improvements, based on suggestions that she received during the presentation and finalized the strategy. She justified all the numbers in the strategy with a revenue model for Powerhouse, which was now beginning to look more and more realistic. Vinod was clear from the beginning that they must develop a market led, financially viable model. He was opposed to the idea of a charity dependent model, which he knew would not have the desired impact.

The Rich Labourer

5

Sustainability

Although by now Vinod had got a good grip on the nuances of Project Powerhouse, he was quite clear that, as a firm, they would like to stay focused on their expertise in finance and audits, and not diversify into housing. He had started this initiative only because he felt a genuine desire from inside to do something for society at large. He seemed to have imbibed this philanthropic streak from his family. His grandfather was a freedom fighter cum businessman, who had given away much of his wealth towards helping people in the heydays during India's struggle for freedom from the British. Vinod's father continued the

The Rich Labourer

philanthropic tradition; however he seemed to lack his grandfather's business acumen and failed miserably in multiple businesses that he attempted. Vinod, as a kid, had seen a fair amount of ups and downs in his family's fortunes. Unlike his previous generations, he took to studies seriously as he and his father realized that education was what could give them security and a stable future. Vinod excelled in his studies, was very good with numbers from his young days, and had built a good reputation and a very good practice as a chartered accountant. He now had forty employees working for him. He took good care of his employees and was genuine in his caring and kind nature towards them and towards people in general.

Vinod wanted to establish proof of concept and help craft a sustainable business model around Powerhouse. He hoped that the team would be able to find the right partners to carry the mission forward. By now he was more convinced than ever that this initiative had the potential to uplift a lot of people socio-economically. Villagers would be able to skill themselves in the erection of Powerhouse and earn additional income thereof. Where grid access was possible, the new net-metering policy of the government would allow homeowners to sell back excess power generated, back to the grid, and earn money. By allowing the end users income generation opportunities from Powerhouse, it would make them stakeholders in the project. Vinod believed that this would be a ground-up movement, as against the conventional trickle down approach for social projects, followed in India, for many years. Besides the net metering policy, other policy changes fueling social innovation were encouraging. There was also an apparent change in people's attitude, as an ecosystem supporting social innovation was fast emerging in the country.

He realized that although Riya's funding strategy would get them through the pilot stage, they would need a long term revenue strategy to firstly find the right partners and secondly to have maximum impact. Vinod took out time over weekends to work on a long-term strategy and discuss the same with Riya over the week. In one such meeting, Riya asked,

"What about copy cats Vinod? Our team has worked so hard on this for months. At the end of it, if people see a working solution, they will quickly copy us."

"More the merrier, Riya. One solution cannot alone address the issues that we are trying to address in a nation of our size. We will need more players."

"I agree; but it's our hard work. It is our intellectual property."

"We will protect the intellectual property under the existing laws. On the business side, we can adopt a licensing model.

The Rich Labourer

People are lax on doing R&D and would rather copy an idea, which works. Powerhouse can be licensed out to multiple players for quick scalability and impact. So we let them copy, but they pay for it!"

"Hmm….that makes a lot of sense. Like the McDonalds of housing!"

Riya often marveled at Vinod's analogous imagination. He could quickly draw inspiration from the strategy of a successful product or service and apply that learning onto a completely different product or service.

Using analogy to spur creative thinking can be fun. It is about applying an out-of-context concept to the problem that one is trying to solve. A visit to a Honda car showroom may sound silly, while designing a house for the poor. But one may discover a memorable customer experience and help in isolating parts of the experience to be applied onto the original design challenge. For example, how can the daunting task of securing finance for a house in India be improved from learnings about the smooth process of car financing? Moreover getting out of the box into a new setting is always a good way to spur creativity.

A long-term revenue strategy began to emerge wherein the intellectual property would be retained by the parent entity. The parent entity would continue to work on product development, product updates, quality management and training. Licensees would deliver

Powerhouse at a local level, through a combination of manufacturing facilities, aggregators, installers and after-sales service personnel. The parent entity would earn from a combination of license fee and a share of sales revenue. The licensee would earn from sales and after-sales service and would also help generate income for the local populace by employing locals in the installation and after-sales teams.

Once this long-term strategy was thought through, Riya volunteered to put the nuts and bolts in place. She further discussed it with her team, detailed it out and put hard numbers onto it. It was looking like a win-win for all now. They had to get the live prototype built now and proof of concept established.

Monitoring & Performance Parameters

Riya was keen to get the live prototype built quickly; as that would give them a shot at exploring a pilot in Rampur. The villagers had contributed much to the project so far and the team felt that they owed it to them. They were anxious to know how they would react to see the product that they had helped develop. Would it really work for them? How would they know?

The team wanted to establish the ways of measuring the performance of Powerhouse. Everything looked hunky dory on paper, but what parameters would they use to measure the desired impact?

In some cases this is easy, and one just has to figure out if a product or service is making money or not. In cases, which have a socio-economic angle to it, it is not only about making money. With help from Ravi, Kishan and Sukanya, Riya began to think about the monitoring and performance parameters for a pilot. She understood that this would be an evolving process and hoped that a specialized team would be able to build upon such indicators once the project was commercialized.

In any project, it is important to establish what purpose such monitoring would serve. Would it establish impact, would it help secure funding or would it help make more money? Data used may help qualitative as well as quantitative measurements and, if of specialized nature, may often call for the inclusion of external experts in the team.

Riya took a prototyping approach to setting up the parameters, with the understanding that the model may be altered for maximum impact, based on the information captured. Keeping a pilot at Rampur in mind, what emerged was a judicious mix of qualitative and quantitative parameters. For the live prototype, the team decided to start with more of the quantitative measurements and hoped to explore the qualitative aspects during the pilot stage. The team decided to incorporate the latest of monitoring tools including sensors and IP enabled devices to keep a tab on the performance of the live prototype over a time range. Data sheets were drawn up to measure time, frequency and other incidents.

Way to Market

Over the next few weeks the live prototype was built in Badlapur. Although it was built on the basis of drawings and documents detailing out the smallest of design and erection methodology, iterations on the fly were done as unexpected, on-ground realities popped up. Every stage of the live prototype was documented using a mix of notes, photography and videography. Upon completion, they began to monitor the performance of the house using the pre-determined parameters.

Upon Ravi's suggestion, Team Powerhouse decided to call a small group of Rampur's inhabitants, to come and have a look at the live prototype. Their valuable feedback was sought. The team also sought feedback from some of the industry experts that they had spoken to earlier. The house was also shown to a few experts who had never heard about the initiative earlier in order to eliminate any bias in the feedback.

The manufacturing of the various components of the live prototype and their erection on site had gone off without major glitches. The team was happy that months of research and planning had paid off. Now they began to take all the feedback they were getting and made iterations as and where required. No feedback, however trivial it may

The Rich Labourer

have sounded, was taken lightly, and was deliberated upon before accepting or rejecting it.

Vinod was very happy with the results. Although he was beginning to wonder if they were spending too much time on Powerhouse, he gave the go-ahead for a pilot at Rampur after minor but necessary iterations were done, based on the feedback received so far. Pravin, an inhabitant of Rampur, was in the process of building a new house on his plot and had budgeted some money for it. Team Powerhouse proposed to have a pilot done on his plot and to cover the additional funds, over and above his budget, if any. Pravin had already seen the live prototype at Badlapur and readily agreed, as he would save much of his time and effort. This would also give the team a chance to monitor the house's performance and impact in a real-world situation, as Pravin would be living in it with his wife and two small kids.

In no time, the first Powerhouse came up in Rampur, and soon Pravin and his family had shifted into it. The team was now tracking progress quantitatively and qualitatively through their pre-determined parameters. Their strategy for the data collection and which metrics were most important, had undergone some changes, based on the feedback received from the live prototype at Badlapur.

The team was now beginning to understand the impact of Powerhouse. Comparing such outcomes with the baseline established in the beginning gave Riya and team a way to assess if they were likely to have the impact that they wanted.

It had been eighteen months now, and all the hard work seemed to be paying off. Although they had tried to keep the work under wraps, word has passed around, and Powerhouse was getting some publicity. All kinds of enquiries began to come in. Some rich individuals wanted them to build it as a farmhouse, some rural folk wanted it for their use, home-builders wanted to use it for their projects, investors wanted more details, potential partners called.

Vinod was happy. He realized that all this attention and the feedback received meant that the solution had a fairly high chance of causing the impact that they wanted. The time was now ripe to hand over the solution to the world. Over the next few weeks, he and Riya negotiated with a few potential partners for setting up a legal entity to run Powerhouse as envisaged. Sukanya, Ravi and Kishan would be the first line of management in the new entity. The students of Architecture, who had been involved from the beginning, had graduated. Some of them would be absorbed in the new entity. Although a lot of potential investors and partners showed interest, Vinod was careful in his selection. He had been in business long enough to understand that, unless the other side had a vision similar to theirs, about impacting lives positively, things may not work out. This was not just another business where you invest with the hope of hyper growth and high valuation.

Eventually they signed up with the new infrastructure division of a large conglomerate, who brought in the required funds into the business. Vinod used his financial acumen and ensured that he and key team members who had helped shape Powerhouse had some equity in the new entity. VM Associates stayed on board the new entity, as financial consultants.

Powerhouse began to steam ahead.

6

Inspiration

"Ding dong! Ding dong!" the doorbell rang as Keerat recognized the standard practice of Neil ringing it twice.

"Coming, coming, beta." Keerat said out loud as she approached the door.

Keerat opened the door and was surprised to see Riya standing next to Neil and Garima.

"Riya? What happened? Is everything allright?" Keerat quizzed.

"Oh I think I forgot to mention to you Maaji; we have a small get-together today; so I came home to change."

It was six months since the reigns of Powerhouse were handed over to the new partners and two years since they had begun work at VM Associates. The key members of the original team and the new team had decided to cut a cake and have dinner together to celebrate two years of Powerhouse that evening. Pankaj had promised to come early, by 6 pm, to take care of the kids in Keerat's absence. It was a Friday, and for a change, Pankaj was looking forward to spending some quality time with Neil and Garima.

It was rare for Pankaj to be spending time with the kids during weekdays. On the way home, he stopped by at a sports store and bought a carrom striker. Neil loved to play carrom, but had lost the striker and was overjoyed when Pankaj showed him the new striker. Pankaj got Keerat and Garima to join in and the four of them spent some quality time playing several games, interspersed with some munchies that Keerat kept serving.

Riya returned a little before midnight, silently opened the door with her key, and was surprised to see Pankaj working on his laptop in the living room.

"Why are you still working? Have the kids slept?" Riya settled next to Pankaj on the sofa, trying to catch his glance.

"Yes, they slept just a while back." Pankaj continued to gaze into the laptop screen.

"Is everything allright?" Riya put her hand through Pankaj's thick hair. She was concerned, as on other days like this, Pankaj would usually welcome her with a smile.

"Yes dear, everything is fine now." Pankaj shut the laptop down, kept it on the coffee table and smiled at Riya.

"Had fun with the kids?"

"Yes, we played carrom, did a bit of homework…and also broke two glasses…"

Riya simply smiled, admiring Pankaj's voluntary act of taking care of the kids every so often, when both were well aware about how much he struggled with it.

"How was the party Riya? In fact I was thinking about Powerhouse."

"It was good. I think everyone liked getting together as a team after all this while. What were you thinking about Powerhouse?"

"How is it going? I mean, you guys did a wonderful job for eighteen months. Then it was passed on to someone else. How did the transition go? Has it been accepted by the end users?"

The Rich Labourer

"We are quite happy from what we have been seeing lately. Fifteen homes have been built in Rampur so far, and the initial feedback is good"

"I have been thinking about the user experience factor. I wonder if the user experience has been designed well enough by the new team." Pankaj wondered.

"You mean the experience journey map? Why? What is your concern?" Riya was a bit puzzled now.

"No, no concern about Powerhouse. I was thinking about experience journey mapping in general. Then I began to relate it to my work and how things could improve."

"Your work? Why…what is wrong Pankaj?" Riya was concerned now.

"Aw…nothing really. Anyway, its too late….lets get some sleep."

"No no no…Pankaj, I am curious now…." Riya insisted.

"Well, it's like this. We run our call centres and BPOs in three shifts. Many of the agents have to fake an accent and work the graveyard shift. They handle complaints from customers in a different country, while putting up an act that they are in the same country. I mean this is the worst case; the point is that we sign contracts with product manufacturers and our agents handle complaints related to products that someone else had designed. For the customer at the other end, a call on the helpline is one of the critical, make-or-break touch points in his or her experience journey of the product. There would be other touch-points in the journey, some of which would be human, like a salesperson or an after-sales service professional. Compared to non-human touch points in the journey, like websites, human touch points have a higher level of inconsistency…because of the simple reason that we are all born unequal. This inconsistency is a problem area. So while training brings in consistency to a fairly high level, an organization usually does not have much control on the human's mind….on his personal life and what he or she is thinking. However when someone is at work, he is largely influenced by his surroundings, by the people around him or her…and I feel, also by the physical space around him."

Pankaj paused. Riya nodded her understanding.

"So, for example, we have seen that, when we have high cubicle partitions, agents become less social and smile less, whereas in more 'open' environments where agents can see each other, they are smiling and socializing better…and this impacts their behavior with clients. The kind of lighting in the office makes a difference, the temperature makes a difference, the level of oxygen makes a difference and I have seen changes in behavior on account of all of these. For us, our biggest investment is in people. Our second biggest investment is in the space and the furniture and fittings, to house these people. While a lot of thinking

The Rich Labourer

and policies are made around the 'human' resources, there is hardly any fresh thinking around the 'non-human' resources. Now, I see that as a problem. If the environment within which these 'human' resources work, does not allow them to perform at their optimum best, they will create a problem in the experience journey of the end user. And when this happens, the product manufacturer will not be seen in the best of light. That's not a win-win situation."

Riya continued to look at Pankaj, expecting more.

"You get my point Riya?" Pankaj asked.

"So you are saying that designing the user experience is as important as designing the product or the service?"

"Exactly! But I am more concerned about improving the performance of our agents; they are our first customers. If we can keep them happy, then they can keep our client's customers happy."

"Hmm…." Riya wondered.

Pankaj continued "We have such high attrition rates despite the best of HR policies, so I have been thinking that we must work on the NHR policies now. I mean the non-human resources, which help the human resources perform."

"Do you think productivity is an issue here?"

The Rich Labourer

"Well, we are at par with industry standards. But I think the industry bar itself can be raised. I am thinking of running a small experiment to test this hypothesis. Anyway, we will talk more on this later. Lets get some sleep now"

Pankaj was in the midst of setting up a new BPO in Pune. It would be for 1000 people. He had proposed to the CEO that while setting up the new centre, he would like to have some of his theories about increased productivity tested. He requested that out of the 1000 agents, they set up an experimental space for 50 agents. This 50 people space would be set up with newer elements that were assumed to raise the productivity bar; 50 agents would be made to work from this space and their productivity levels would be tested and compared with another 50 working in the 'regular' space. As it did not involve any major cost increase, his CEO had agreed.

The Rich Labourer

7

The 3P method in organisations

That a better workplace environment produces better results is an accepted assumption. In general, different workplaces are designed differently, and this is because of the different nature of jobs that will happen within the spaces. For example, a Call Centre design is very different from an Investment Banker's workplace design. In corporate organisations, HR managers measure performance of employees by way of output by employees, which is related to productivity. While productivity is influenced by factors like technology, organisation's vision, employees; it is also dependent on the physical environment and its effect on health and employees' performance.

This holds true in any working environment, be it a corporate office or a factory. In a factory setting, it is easier to measure output, as there are tangible measurement parameters. In factories productivity can be measured by the number of units produced per employee per hour or per shift. In a corporate office setting, subjective performance measurements may be used, where a mix of structured questionnaires and observation techniques may be used. Such data may be collected from employees, supervisors, clients, customers and suppliers to measure productivity.

An independent research firm conducted a research on workplace environments (Gensler, 2006) in the United States. In March 2006, a survey was conducted by taking a sample size of 2013. The research was related to workplace designs, work satisfaction, and productivity. 89 percent of the respondents rated design, from important to very important. Almost 90 percent of senior officials revealed that effective workplace design is important for the increase in employees' productivity. The final outcome of the survey suggested that businesses could enhance their productivity by improving their workplace designs. A rough estimation was made by executives, which showed

The Rich Labourer

that almost 22 percent increase could be achieved in an organisation's performance if their offices were well designed.

But practically, many organizations still do not give much importance to workplace design. As many as 40 percent of the employees believe that their companies want to keep their costs low, that is why their workplaces have bad designs; and 46 percent of employees think that the priority list of their company does not have workplace design on top. When data was summarized, almost one out of every five employees rated their workplace environment from, 'fair to poor'. 90 percent admitted that their attitude about work is adversely affected by the quality of their workplace environment. Yet again 89 percent blamed their working environment for their job dissatisfaction.

₹₹₹

During the course of her work on Powerhouse, Riya used to often talk with Pankaj and update him about the progress. It was an exciting time for her and she got to learn much during those eighteen months. On a couple of occasions, Pankaj had met some of the team members as well. He had also heard much about the leadership role that Ravi had played within the team, to drive the work around the spatial design of Powerhouse. He realized that he would need someone like Ravi in his team, who would be willing to challenge conventions by way of research, which could prove bold hypothesis. He had met a few other Architects

The Rich Labourer

and Interior Designers on the topic and was not overly happy with what he had seen so far.

One day, he met up for lunch with Ravi on this. Halfway through Pankaj's briefing, Ravi said abruptly,

"Count me in Pankaj! When do we begin?"

He could well connect with Pankaj's thought process. Ravi, after all, was a firm believer in the direct impact of physical environment on human psychology. Soon, Pankaj's team followed due procedure, did a quick techno-commercial bidding for the selection of a consultant. Ravi won the assignment. Within two days of Ravi's appointment, he was sitting in Pankaj's office to kick-start the project.

The 3P method at work

"Lets first understand your people Pankaj."

Ravi was keen to understand the people's needs before they started designing and building the work-area for the sample of 50 agents.

Pankaj was keen to experiment with the sample quickly, but he understood Ravi's focus on human centricity, given his experience in dealing with that aspect. He had also heard much about the gains in Powerhouse by following that method. So they decided to follow the 3P method and divide the project into the following stages:

The Rich Labourer

- Probe: Understand what the employees want
- Ponder: Synthesize the data to come up with new ideas on the workplace environment
- Prove: Build the pilot like Pankaj suggested with 50 employees

Pankaj laid down the purpose of the experiment: To find out the relationship between office design and employees' productivity and the impact of office design on employees' productivity.

He felt that if he could prove his hypothesis, it would not only lead to a completely new blueprint for the development of workplaces at Paceman, but also greatly benefit Paceman's business model itself.

Ravi was quick at getting things organized. He took under his wings a bright young intern, Mishika, who had joined his team recently. With her help, he quickly framed the questionnaires as well as the observation methodologies to be followed to run the exercise during the probe stage. For the sake of generating inclusive insights, they decided to consider a sample spread across the Pune, Hyderabad and Gurgaon centres. This would give a good diversity within the sample.

Pankaj was keen to get things started sooner than later and initially he questioned the need to consider multiple cities for the study. He soon gave in to Ravi's confidence and realized that it was important to get as diverse insights as possible, even from within standardized frameworks.

Ninety employees were taken as the sample size from the three centres, and it was a healthy mix of agents, team leaders and managers. A mix of one-to-one structured interviews, group interviews and observation techniques using photography and videography were used to collect information about the behavior of employees as well as the workplace design. Even security camera feeds were studied to observe behavior.

A structured questionnaire was used to collect primary data. From the twenty-eight questions in it, there were five on productivity. A subjective productivity measurement technique was used for these questions and such data was collected from the employees as well as from clients and suppliers. Respondents were asked to rate productivity levels on a scale of one to five.

Building It

Furniture, noise, temperature, lighting and spatial arrangement were considered as indicators of office design which affected productivity and the response for each was measured. The data thus collected was analysed to determine respective factors for decreased productivity and understand the extent of the loss in productivity.

A primary factor, which affected employee productivity, was lighting. Spatial arrangement was the other important factor, followed by factors like noise, furniture and temperature. Natural light played a crucial role and the presence or absence of it affected employees in different ways. Moreover poor artificial lighting reduced productivity of employees.

A direct relationship between office design and productivity was becoming obvious.

It was now evident that due importance was not being given to office design as a crucial factor in increasing employees' productivity. Pankaj was surprised to know that 42 percent of employees believed that the workplace had bad designs because they wanted to keep their costs low. 90 percent admitted that their attitude about work is adversely affected by the quality of their workplace environment while 80 percent considered that the working environment was a reason for their job dissatisfaction. Pankaj was staring at this and much more raw data, some of which were difficult to digest. What he had suspected all along, now had data to support the hypothesis. The findings were also a very good starting point for them to work on the design of the pilot space with fifty employees in the upcoming Pune centre.

Two colleagues assisted Mishika during the fact-finding stage; she did a good job of putting all the findings together in the form of a preliminary report. This was the starting

The Rich Labourer

point for Ravi to start work on the design principles for the live prototype. Unlike other design assignments where clients would demand that Architects design what they want, Ravi was excited that he had data to back up the design principles. The availability of such data made it easy for him to think objectively. Design, after all, is about problem solving.

It had been four months since they began. The new centre in Pune was now open. Much as he wanted, Pankaj could not stall the start of the centre till the results of the study were known, due to client commitments. He had conducted a separate bidding process to select the consultants and contractors for the design of the larger space. He kept aside an area of four thousand square feet for them to do the live prototype for fifty employees. It had taken a lot for Pankaj to convince his management to agree to the needs of his experiments. He was now happy that the results so far seemed to be supportive of his calculated risk. He also realized that it was rare to find such support and he had a lot at stake. It was now time to demonstrate.

Over the next twelve weeks, Ravi went back and forth with Pankaj to finalise the design for the live prototype. Although things happened at a frenetic pace, the overall duration was longer than during a conventional design process. They were challenging conventions within the design itself, and getting the nuances of these right was taking time. They had to be absolutely sure. Ravi coordinated with a network of product manufacturers, lighting consultants, electrical engineers, green consultants, aircon experts and others during this period. Pankaj was surprised to realize that many of the product manufacturers were involved in valuable R&D in their efforts to come up with efficient products, which reduced human effort and increased productivity. Such efforts never came to the surface due to a combination of such manufacturers' sales team's overzealous focus on sales as well as the seemingly meaningless rush within client organisations to build new workplaces like instant coffee.

One of the findings was that air quality made a substantial difference in the performance of the agents, and Ravi was keen to ensure that small details like this were handled with care to ensure that it had a positive outcome on the employees' productivity. He wanted the right percentage of oxygen in the air within the workplace. The design was finalized to this level of detailing, covering all aspects.

"Wow, that's a whole lot of drawings Ravi!" exclaimed Pankaj.

Ravi had come to present the final set of drawings to Pankaj before construction could start. They had finalized building services consultants necessary for the project and Ravi had consolidated all the drawings from each of these consultants as well as his drawings, for a sign-off from Pankaj. The number of drawings was well over one hundred.

The Rich Labourer

"I have never seen so many drawings for a project." continued Pankaj.

"Well, if this is successful, I am sure we can standardize many of these drawings, so that we have fewer print-outs for future projects." Ravi was planning to create a standardization manual as part of his project report, at the end of the project. The project was scheduled to run for six months after it was occupied, to monitor the performance of the employees and then to compare the results, with results from the other section.

Contractors were finalized through a bidding process and work progressed quickly as no time was lost in design or specification clarifications. Everything was on paper and easy to understand. Pankaj had hired a project management consultant to monitor the progress of the work. The project managers aligned their standard procedures with some of the unique parameters laid down by Ravi's team. Contrary to traditional practices, over eighty percent of the furniture and fittings were manufactured off-site in the controlled environment of factories. This brought about quality consistency and reduced erection time drastically.

In six weeks, the space was ready to be occupied.

"Wow, this looks better than on paper!" Pankaj's CEO Patrick said upon inspection of the new premises. Three-dimensional imagery, using virtual reality tools were used during the design stage and shared with Patrick.

"Thanks Patrick; but we have to get the people to sit here and see if it really works". Pankaj was quite clear in his mind that it was not only about looks anymore. Spaces could look very beautiful, but what really mattered was how they worked on the minds of the humans who worked within them.

Proving It

The space was soon filled in with the planned fifty employees and began to operate as an independent BPO unit. Fifty employees with matching professional parameters were identified from the adjacent larger section of the unit, and employee productivity was measured for six months for both of these samples. The human resources department led the monitoring with periodical reporting to Pankaj. Ravi's team did observation studies of both the sections.

At the end of six months, Ravi initiated a questionnaire led study to cover both the samples. The questions were extensions of the questionnaire-based study done during the initial phase, in order to determine change in responses, if any. The findings for the new space were compared with the findings for the adjacent space as well with the original findings. Pankaj now knew that the findings would give a jolt to management:

- **Air Quality**: Poor air quality could lower performance by up to 10%. These were measured on parameters as typing speed and calls handled. Sick leave was found to be 30% lower in the new smaller space, which was better ventilated with outdoor air supply, as compared to the larger space. When extrapolated in rupee terms, the lower productivity, absences from work amounted to a Rs. 75,000 per employee per year loss.

- **Daylighting**: This is the practice of placing windows and reflective surfaces so that during the day natural light provides effective internal lighting. The new space was designed with this in mind and had a better view of the outside; allowing ample natural light to flow in. The agents in the new space were found to be processing calls 7% to 12% faster when they had the best possible view of the outside, when compared to those in the other centres with no view. Tests of mental function and memory recall showed that that agents with a view of the outside performed 10% to 25% better than those without a view. Daylighting was also saving 30% on the electricity bill for Pacemen.

- **Ergonomics**: Poor ergonomics was seen to be costing Paceman a loss of Rs. 115,000 per employee per year. This was due to lower productivity and higher incidences of sick leaves. Bad office ergonomics in the existing centres had issues that were impacting the overall health of employees. Common issues included wrong heights for table and chairs, knees banging on keyboard trays, cramped spaces, lack of back and elbow support, elbows resting on hard surfaces.

There were many more similar findings, capturing the effects of colours, temperature, humidity, noise and others. Low temperature levels were a major factor in lower productivity due to the inability to concentrate on account of lower body heat and shivering. Soft background instrumental music was seen to be aiding agents who were tackling claims from impatient customers, as the music helped in relaxing the mind. On the other hand, hard noise from telephone rings and loud conversations were adversely affecting the performance.

Ravi prepared a Project Report, which documented not only the findings but also gave a detailed blueprint for the future. It gave benchmarks for future facilities based on the findings and standards to be followed. None of it was based on hearsay, but on the real needs of real people within their organization.

Over the next three years, Pankaj was tasked to incorporate the recommended changes across all centres. He adopted different strategies for existing and new premises for smooth integration. During this period, the organization saw substantial improvement in their staff's happiness quotient and in their productivity, demonstrating a correlation between the two. The human resources department accepted the fact that the working environment can have a very high impact on productivity. This altered conventional thinking and human resources policies were altered to incorporate the new thinking.

Outstanding customer service and customer experience can only be provided by employees who feel happy and engaged at work.

When employees are happy, so are customers. And when customers are happy, they become loyal to brands. They spend more and more money with the brand, leading to increased profits.

Pankaj's organization was in the business of providing customer service to consumers of large global brands. Soon the positive effect on the bottom-line of such brands was becoming visible. This, in turn, led to high growth levels for Paceman.

After three years, the management at Paceman was making plans to accommodate 25% year on year growth. The management prepared a three-year plan; among other things, it showed plans for four more centres, some located even in neighbouring countries.

A 25% year on year growth sounded heavy for Pankaj's shoulders. He felt he had done his bit for Paceman, and now prepared to pursue his other dreams.

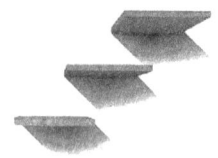

8

Designing Experiences

Happy employees mean happy customers. However, in the journey of the customer's experience with a brand, he encounters human, as well as non-human touch points. It is critical that customers have a positive experience at each touch point, so that they keep coming back.

Each touch point has layers, with only the surface layer being visible to the customers. So when a customer of, say Brand X, has a happy experience with a customer care executive on the phone, it only demonstrates the high level of precision which has gone behind designing and

The Rich Labourer

executing that touch point. Brand X might have taken a 3P approach to arrive at a decision to outsource calls, and through another bidding process would have selected Paceman. Paceman went to great lengths to make sure that Brand X's customers were happy at the end of the calls they made. In a similar fashion, a non-human touch point like a mobile app for the same brand, would involve multiple layers below the user-interface on a cellphone screen. Meticulous detailing goes behind designing the layers of each touch point of successful brands.

Multiple touch points in the journey map of the customer often happen to be inter-related to each other. So designing the co-relation between different touch points is critical and often is a make-or-break aspect of experience design. Designing the entire experience journey for the customer is experience design. It includes all the experiences that precede or follow the actual consumption of a product or a service.

In case of Pankaj, he had helped re-design the experience of their internal customer, their employees. New human resources policies incorporated all the learnings from Pankaj's study to adopt human centricity and to ensure that employees had positive experiences at every touch point in their experience journey on a day-to-day basis with Paceman.

On the other hand, Riya had effected the development of a novel solution. Novel solutions, in turn, mean a completely new way that a customer will engage with a brand. In case of Powerhouse, it meant that customers would get a totally new experience of owning a home or addressing their power needs. Such innovations call for designing the user experience from scratch, and are often more challenging than in case of a product or service, which undergoes incremental improvements.

The demonetization of five hundred and one thousand Indian Rupee notes in 2016 is an example of how a change in the experience journey can impact lives. Without warning, the Government of India announced that these two currency bills would have no legal tender. This action completely changed the way people looked at money, and the experience that people had with money on a day-to-day basis. Overnight, conventional money related touch points either disappeared or changed. Plastic money came to the fore as did other online modes of payments. People had to adapt to a new way of leading their lives as the experience journey map changed. The suddenness of the announcement was like a reset button; imagine how your experience with your computer or smartphone changes after you hit the 'reset to factory settings' button. People's money was safe, they just had to adapt to a new experience journey map. Despite the initial problems people faced, the move received support from all sections, as it promised to tackle three major malaises plaguing the Indian economy—a parallel economy, counterfeit currency in circulation and terror financing.

Experience Design Management

Truly path-breaking innovations are rare, and in no time they too get copied. The world is commoditized today and everything is quite similar to each other. We have similar products, similar services, similar technology and similar pricing. In such a world, the difference lies in the perception; the difference lies in the branding. The 'feel' about a brand is delivered through customer experiences and value is created. Value is no more created at the product level on the shop floor, but co-created today by customers, during touch points in the experience journey.

Experience design management is thus the conceptualization, development and orchestration of all interactions between a customer and a brand over time. This is done to maximize value generation both for the customer as well as for the brand. Take the example of a visitor to a Starbucks. Coffee is sold at double digit multiples after covering cost, because of the perceived value. As a customer goes through various touch points in his journey from thinking about a coffee, through having it in Starbucks, to reflecting after he or she finishes it, the customer is passively and actively involved in the value creation process. In such a journey, some experiences are cognitive, some emotional and some are simple. Some are make-or-break touch points, the outcome of which will determine if the customer will come back or not. Positive customer experiences at every touch point are important to produce brand loyalty, and give brands competitive advantage.

Experience centres are commonplace today. These are centres where customers can get to experience products, touch them and feel them. Given the broader definition of experience design, such experience centres are only one of the touch points in the journey map of the customer. Such centres can often be make-or-break touch points and serve to expedite customer acquisition time.

An experience happens whenever a customer comes into contact with a brand across all touch points; to the extent that a customer cannot not have an experience.

Product companies today focus on the experience by customers; or rather by humans. Experience design thus embraces the emotional and imaginary elements of an experience. Humans do not buy products because of the product's efficiency or utility value alone; experience design thus addresses the hedonic psychology of experiences.

Standardisation

Pankaj's clients had been large product and services companies. Such clients would outsource their customer care services to a specialised organization like Paceman. As

The Rich Labourer

part of the onboarding process, training is imparted to the agents by the client organization. Such training is held at periodic intervals to maintain quality consistency and to keep the agents updated about the latest products and services. When a customer journey map is drawn at the Client origanisations' end, it is important that efforts are made to standardize each touch point, such that end users experience consistent quality every time, and they keep coming back. However, much as they try, client organisations do not always have 100% control over each touch point, especially the outsourced ones. In case of Pankaj's client organisations, they were lucky to have signed up with an organization like Paceman, who went to great lengths to drive productivity excellence. But this does not happen every time. It is not uncommon to hear of organisations giving inconsistent experiences at a touch point due to poor performance by an outsourced partner.

Product manufacturers go to great lengths in their standardization efforts to ensure that end users have consistent positive experiences. However, it is not always within their control. Take the example of aerated drinks, where most popular brands are available widely, from fancy restaurants to highway shops. The outlets where end-users buy and consume such drinks are usually seen as the last mile in the journey. To ensure consistent positive experiences for end users at this last mile, product manufacturers of such brands specify storage norms for such drinks; at what temperature such drinks need to be stored, for how long and so on. Despite such strict norms, experiments have shown that the same drink or food tastes very different when the physical environment changes. The experience of consuming a Coke and Lays wafers at an Indian highway shop will be very different from consuming the same in a fancy restaurant.

In case of certain products like McDonalds burgers where standardization is key, the focus is on ensuring that the customer gets a positive experience even at the last mile. So not only are the store design manuals standardized to the smallest of detailing; the parent organization would often be involved in the design and execution of the stores also. McDonalds customers across the world walk into any new McDonalds store with a high degree of familiarity about the store experience. Familiarity about touch points brings in comfort in the end users' mind. Such comfort usually keeps them from avoiding unfamiliar competitors, even if they have better burgers. This increases the brand value for McDonalds.

When Architects and Interior Designers are given design briefs for a new project, rarely do clients brief them or hand over a report highlighting the reasoning behind a certain 'look and feel' that the client needs them to deliver. After organisations follow the 3P method to innovate new products and services, the next thing is to map the customer experience journey. Some of the touch points are co-created with third parties. The more an Architect or

The Rich Labourer

Interior Designer gets to know about the results of a 3P initiative, the more likely he or she will come up with a design, which will be in sync with the expected experience of an end user at that touch point. In the absence of such knowledge the Architect or the Interior Designer is likely to use the opportunity given by the assignment to design another space, which will win them another award, but may do nothing to stir the customers' souls.

This is true about all other agencies which help to co-create experience touch points. A creative agency, which is assigned to generate online content or generate advertisement creatives or figure out a brand strategy, will be grappling in the dark, unless they fully understand the ethos behind a product and what it means to the consumer. Such an agency needs to be given access to the 3P report if it exists. A 3P report is like the Holy Grail and is a starting point for the design of every touch point in the customer experience journey.

The 3P method is not only for organizations though. It is for people as well.

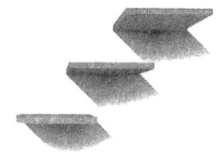

9

For a better self

The 3P Method for a Better Self

"I think it's about time." said Pankaj as Riya opened the door for him.

It was 10.30 pm on a Friday and Pankaj had just returned from work. He was mentally exhausted after a hectic week, replete with multiple internal meetings with Paceman's stakeholders, as they planned for growth over the next three years. The kids had gone to sleep, and Riya had burrowed herself into the recliner in the living room, with a novel. The recliner that Pankaj mostly sat on, to watch

The Rich Labourer

television or read the newspaper had grown soft over the years, from regular use as well as Garima jumping on it like a trampoline in her early years.

"Time for what Pankaj?" Riya was puzzled and wondered what Pankaj had in mind at this late hour.

Pankaj instinctively headed for the recliner and sank in. He didn't say anything as he began to remove his shoes. Riya was concerned now.

"What is it Pankaj?"

"I think we have to make the jump now. We need to start our own consultancy; I have had enough of coming home so late."

"Yes, I agree Pankaj."

Although it had been on Pankaj and Riya's mind over the last few years, over the last few months, the need to leave the corporate race was felt more than ever. Although he was well compensated, Pankaj's workload had increased manifold. He was spending more and more time at work and hardly getting any time at home. If weekends were not spent at work, he would continuously be on phone. Pankaj's stress levels were high, and he had gained a lot of weight over the last three years. He recently got a health scare when his blood pressure showed some abnormal readings and the doctor had advised him to reduce weight, do regular exercise and get more sleep. Now Paceman management was planning a massive expansion drive; this would mean that things would only get worse for Pankaj.

He had money, but felt poor.

On the other hand, Riya's workload was much easier. The nature and pace of work that Vinod was in, ensured regular work from dedicated clients. VM Associates signed up on annual basis with clients, which ensured regular income flow. Clients would not leave them unless there was a major goof-up, which was rare. Word of mouth helped positive growth; Vinod had however found his sweet spot in an optimum team size of 40-50 staff. This allowed him to generate good revenues and needed him to spend just about the right amount of time on company affairs, while still allowing him to pursue other interests which appealed to his heart. This is how Powerhouse had emerged and he had instilled the same belief in his staff, most of who were with him for several years now. He took good care of them, financially and gave them enough room to spend quality time with their family and other personal interests.

Building a Future Together

Riya and Pankaj had often discussed about relocating to the relatively less busy city of Pune. With the kids growing up fast, they felt that they would be able to give them a better quality of life in Pune. The city still had ample open spaces and traffic was still manageable. It was culturally very rich, they had relatives there and most importantly the

The Rich Labourer

city had some very good schools. They felt that they would be able to spend more time together as a family in a city like that. Over the last three years, Pankaj hardly saw his children. Relocating to Pune would not be a very difficult plan to execute. They had invested in a large apartment in a good locality, which was now ready for occupancy. The apartment was part of a large complex, and faced the Mula Mutha river. Pankaj would often dream of a day when he would sit on the balcony, facing the river, sipping coffee while reading a newspaper or working on his laptop.

Pankaj wanted to quit his job and become a strategic innovation consultant. He felt that he had learned enough in his two decades journey of the corporate world, to be in a position to consult corporations privately. The story of how he had effected a positive change in productivity at Paceman, by following the 3P method, had been circulated in the electronic and print media. People had heard about his work and he would often get calls from corporate headhunters, offering him new jobs at a much higher salary.

Higher salary was no more a motivator for Pankaj; in between him and Riya, they had invested their earnings well in a mix of real estate, mutual funds and fixed deposits and could live off the earnings of the investments. Their earnings were now working for them. However the headhunters calls confirmed Pankaj's belief that there was a huge opportunity out there to serve multiple corporations as a private consultant.

Riya's work around Powerhouse was well documented and widely published. Pankaj had learned much about the research methodology used in the conceptualization of Powerhouse from Riya, and he had built upon that knowhow to bring about the changes at Paceman. He knew that all of their combined knowledge could be used to develop consultancy and training modules for corporations. Showing people a structured method towards innovation could be his forte.

"You take the plunge first, I will follow" Riya suggested.

Although Pankaj suggested that they should both start the consultancy together, Riya felt that Pankaj should start first and she could join him once revenue inflow was stable. In between the two of them, they had a wealth of knowledge and experience. So working together made sense not only from a business point of view, but they would be great mental supports to each other as well. After all, starting off on their own, after nearly two decades of being in cushy jobs, would not be so easy. But Pankaj had made up his mind now. He quit.

Pankaj's bosses were reluctant and resisted his attempts much. Pankaj explained as best as he could and a mutual agreement was reached to retain Pankaj as a consultant for at least one year. He would be free to pursue other clients

The Rich Labourer

and signed a confidentiality agreement with Paceman. Pankaj was a true professional and would never reveal the findings of his work in one corporation to another.

The plan now was for Pankaj to start the consultancy practice while Riya would retain her job. Once the practice began to earn, Riya would join in and they would relocate to Pune. As private consultants, they could be in any city, which had good connectivity with other major centres, and Pune would work very well.

But Pankaj had other things to take care off. Before he started, he wanted to fix a few other things that required his attention. He needed to lose weight, and now he had the time to do it.

Losing Weight

Eating at odd hours, lack of excercise and stress had taken a toll on Pankaj. Over the last five years he had gained over thirty kgs. He was now a hefty 105 kgs with associated problems like fluctuating blood pressure and fatigue. Pankaj had learned a few tricks over the years about problem defining and problem solving. He now decided to take up the weight loss challenge as one such problem, which needed fixing.

Pankaj began by looking inside himself to define the problem he was trying to solve:

"What will I gain by losing weight?"

The Rich Labourer

By asking this question, he had reframed the problem. Over the years he had tried fancy quick fix diets, but nothing seemed to work. Because he felt lowly about himself because of his weight, he had also stopped socialising with friends, who remembered him as the athletic Pankaj.

So when Pankaj asked himself this question, he was probing. The answers he got surprised him. He realised that he wanted to lose weight because he wanted to feel good about himself and confident to go out and meet friends and socialise. He also wanted to feel less tired.

Reframing helped him realise that the problem was not about losing weight, but about connecting with friends, about getting enough sleep and eating right. So Pankaj bought new clothes to make it easier to socialise. Along with that he also bought some new exercise wear and he began to focus on reconnecting with friends. He began to sleep and get up early. He would get up before dawn and started going out for long walks; the morning fresh air kept him energetic throughout the day.

Free food at the cafeteria at Paceman had made it difficult for Pankaj to resist carbohydrates and sugar. Now he had taken up a serviced office, two kilometres from his house, and he started walking to and fro. As he was now getting all his meals from home, he eliminated sugar and processed carbohydrates and this gave him energy and helped lose weight quickly.

The Rich Labourer

Pankaj began to lose weight, and he felt he was achieving this by doing 'nothing' about weight loss. He had just shifted focus on the real issues which were troubling him all this while; and had made new habits. Building habits is important and is the key to re-inventing oneself.

The new serviced office too had a cafeteria with a good spread of food. At times when he could not get home food he found some strategies that worked. He began to head instinctively to the salad bar and fill a bowl with salad. He would still have his favourite chicken, but would place it on top of the salad. This way he was filling in less of the greasy stuff than he would if the bowl or plate was empty. He replaced aerated drinks with water.

Willpower is not enough. What helps is habit formation. The habit of waking up at 5 am and going for a walk in the neighborhood park also helped Pankaj meet new walking buddies. Soon he became part of a group which helped him upgrade to shorter runs as he worked on monthly challenges to increase stamina.

By running with a regular group, it helped reinforce the habit. Pankaj went from thinking about walking 1 km was really long and hard, to thinking that was a nice warm-up, because he was jogging with people who ran 8-10 kms every morning.

If one is working hard on a problem and it is not working, then he or she is working on the wrong problem. Reframing the problem makes it easier to solve.

Relocating to Pune

Pankaj and Riya used to romanticize about shifting to Pune and get away from the rush, the noise and the traffic of Mumbai. Now they began to ask themselves:

"What would shifting to Pune do to our family?"

They realized that being in Pune would allow the family to spend quality time together and for the kids to enjoy the outdoors. They felt that the shift would also allow Pankaj and Riya the time and space to focus on their private consultancy while allowing them a healthy lifestyle. It became clear that the shift would do a lot of good to the family as a whole, and individually as well.

Within a year of Pankaj's quitting his job, he had a flourishing consultancy practice. He was much sought after as a trainer as well as a strategic consultant to corporations for their real estate and infrastructure needs. His clients were all across the country and he realized that he could be anywhere in the country and still be as effective; all he needed was an airport with good connectivity.

The Rich Labourer

Soon thereafter, once the kids's school term ended, they relocated to Pune. Although Vinod was initially upset with Riya's decisions, he soon came around as he understood that Riya was doing what her heart was telling her to do, and in that sense she was not very different from the way he was. Vinod also saw this as an opportunity to expand his client base to Pune, and worked out an arrangement with Riya such that she could handle any assignment in Pune. This worked well for Pankaj and Riya as it made the transition easier. Riya could work at her own time and pace, from Pankaj's office in Pune, and that would also involve a variable compensation structure. She felt this was a win win as this would give her time to settle down in Pune and also an opportunity for Vinod to explore the Pune market. Vinod and Riya decided to try this for a year and then evaluate.

The 3P Method in Design Thinking

The 3P Method is aligned with the now hip 'Design Thinking' methodology, which is about using a designer's toolkit to solve real world problems. Most part of an individual's behavior is under his or her control. So in a way, by changing oneself, one can change the world one lives in. The simple question to ask is "What do I want my future self to be?" This sounds quite like a design problem and the 3P method can be applied to solve it, as Pankaj showed.

The Rich Labourer

Pankaj had tried for years to lose weight. He had tried going to the gym at the workplace in the evenings for 30 mins — that didn't work due to his erratic work schedules. He had tried to go for a walk in the mornings before work; that didn't work. He joined a Facebook group of friends to have accountability partners — that didn't work. Then when he reframed the whole thing, it began to work.

It is not about the specific strategies for behavior change — it's about using the 3P method to be more purposeful and systematic in making those changes.

- **Probe**: What do you observe in yourself that is driving your current behavior?

- **Ponder**: What behavior change do you want to create? What different actions do you want to be choosing? What are some different ways you can move towards your goal? What are some quick and easy experiments you can try? Is there something you can do today that will give you an idea of whether the behavior change works for you?

- **Prove**: Which experiments work? What sticks? Then go back to Probe, and think about why certain experiments work better than others? For the ones that don't, is it because this particular experiment doesn't click with you, or is it that the problem definition isn't right?

By being purposeful in designing the person that you want to be, one can bring in a great sense of fulfillment in one's life.

The Rich Labourer

10

For society

Five years after their shift to Pune, Pankaj was a happy and trim self. Professionally he was doing well, and Riya was now actively involved in his work. Riya helped clients develop revenue models for strategies that Pankaj proposed, and she looked after the day-to-day running of the office. They had a team of ten staff, and they found this size to be optimum, allowing them a good work-life

The Rich Labourer

balance. They earned well enough for the kids' education and their future needs.

Garima had started going to junior college now. A student of Symbiosis College, she was a bubbly young girl and a bright student with interests in drama and the arts. One of her classmates was Seema, who was the daughter of Saee, who used to work with her household as a maid in Mumbai. Life had completely turned around for Saee and Ramesh after they had left Mumbai.

Ramesh was no more the poor labourer that we was in Mumbai. He first felt he was no more poor the day he held a debit card. During the Government's push for financial inclusion, following the demonetization drive of high currency notes in 2016, Ramesh had opened a bank account. This gave him a high, as he finally felt included in the greater Indian society. He finally had what only his rich bosses had - a bank account with a debit card. He was no more a castaway. He could take out money from an ATM when he wanted and could save more. He felt he was in control of his money. This gave him confidence and new ideas to improve his family's lives.

Ramesh had his ancesteral home at Shikrapur near Pune. Seven years back he had shifted back to Shikrapur, as new opportunities had opened up near his village. Given the proximity to Pune, the government had begun promoting the region as an industrial belt. Job opportunities had opened up and Ramesh could get a job with a steel factory,

The Rich Labourer

which had opened. The factory was part of an industrial zone that had come up two kilometers away from his village. He was now assured of regular income and other family benefits, which meant more money than his irregular income as a labourer in Mumbai. His expenses were lower. He could live in his spacious family house, surrounded by friends and family. Saee found work as a maid in the residential campus of the factory. They not only began to save a bit of money, but also supplemented their earnings with agricultural income. Ramesh had an acre of ancestral agricultural land, and he leased it out to a family in the village to do farming.

All along, Ramesh and Saee strived to ensure that Seema and Rohit continued to study. The factory had begun a school for its employees, and Seema and Rohit secured good quality education at subsidized rates.

In the meanwhile, Powerhouse had made inroads into remote parts of Maharashtra. Besides other factors, the financial inclusion of large populations across rural areas made it easy for them to secure mortgage finance. Shikrapur did not remain untouched. A delivery unit, which handled installation of Powerhouse units in the surrounding villages, had come up in Shikrapur two years back. Locals were trained to become installers and the popularity of Powerhouse ensured a regular flow of work. Ramesh signed up to become a certified installer under the 'outsourced' category. He could lend his services to the

The Rich Labourer

delivery and installation team during his off hours and off days. This brought the family additional income.

Around the same time, Ramesh also got a Powerhouse for himself, taking advantage of the special discount for Powerhouse staff and installers. As Ramesh had managed to keep his income flow regular, he had a good credit rating with his bank. So securing a loan for Powerhouse was fairly easy for him. Ramesh enrolled under the net-metering scheme and soon they were selling power back to the grid. The net metering policy allowed families to earn from selling back excess power generated from rooftop solar PV systems. They were producing more electricity then they needed, and the payback from the power company was offsetting the loan for the house.

The new house made a world of difference to the family. Earlier they were living in a run down house that Ramesh's father had built thirty years back. It leaked during the rains and got very hot during the summer months. Someone or the other would often fall sick. Living in the new Powerhouse eliminated such trouble. Moreover they were now ensured of continuous power in a region, which saw erratic power cuts. Ramesh had also bought an electric two-wheeler and freed himself from the worries of the rising price of petrol.

Ramesh and Saee ensured that Seema and Rohit were not deprived of good education. They were well aware that a good education would make all the difference in the childrens' life. Seema had done well in studies in school and made her parents very proud when she secured admission in Symbiosis College, one of the best colleges of Pune city. Seema had to travel ninety minutes one-way to reach college, but with reliable bus connectivity, nobody was complaining.

Seema wanted to become an engineer. Rohit wanted to become a pilot. With ten years left in his job, and enough supplementary income, Ramesh did not consider these to be impossible dreams. He felt good about the way life had shaped up. He felt rich.

The Government had made Sikrapur a part of the Greater Pune Metropolitan Region and had much promoted the region as an industrial hub. This was done on the strength of research, which had given the decision makers credible data to base judgement upon. Over the years the area had developed much, and connectivity with Pune had become easy with good roads and frequent buses.

Can the 3P method be used for the holistic development of societies?

3P method for Society

The 3P Method is not only for organisations and for individuals but society can use it to bring about positive change, like the way Powerhouse did. The process is deeply human and so are the results. Rather than a sequential flow, the method is more like a system of overlapping spaces; *probe, ponder, and prove*. One often keeps going back and forth between these spaces till a solution is reached. For those used to milestone-based processes in organisations, the 3P Method can appear a bit chaotic when doing it the first time; but over time participants realize that it makes sense and achieves results. The Probe stage defines the problem or opportunity that motivates the search for solutions; Ponder is the stage during which ideas are generated, developed and tested; Prove is that stage which allows the solution to be deployed among people.

The method allows one to tap into existing capacities that are overlooked by conventional problem-solving methods. At a city and regional level, the administration usually has access to tons of data about existing capacities - data like the number of graduates per year and in which streams, data like the number of skilled labourers, number of scientists in universities and in which fields of work, number of incubation centres, real estate data, etc. Such data can be synthesized and then used to bring about positive changes by way of communicating a city's or region's competitive advantage. This can define whether the city will see growth or decline in the future.

Globally countries compete to attract talent, jobs and investment. Even cities do. For example, India and Phillipines compete to attract global investment in the business of call centres and BPOs. State government

The Rich Labourer

sponsored investment summits have become a trend and states within India compete for investments. Even cities do. In the early eighties, a suburb of Mumbai called Andheri East was the hub of the fledging IT industry in India, with the government promoted SEEPZ (Santacruz Electronic Export Processing Zone) located there. With the Indian economy opening up in the nineties to the world, and with multinational corporations demanding better and bigger infrastructure, the industry quickly shifted to Bengaluru. There was a flight of all IT companies to Bengaluru, from Andheri East. Ever since, other IT hubs have developed in other cities like Pune, Hyderabad and Gurgaon. Unless Bengaluru manages to retain its competitive advantage over other cities, in future, it may lose the tag as the IT capital of India.

Till the early nineties, nearly all FMCG (Fast Moving Consumer Goods) producers used to be headquartered in Mumbai. However with rising price of real estate and failing public infrastructure, the equations changed and several such organisations shifted to other cities, especially Gurugram. Newer Indian organisations and multinational corporations making an entry to India today often start their Indian operations in cities like Gurugram and Bengaluru.

Humans live in cities and their present and future are dependent on the city's performance. Till the time the Lower Parel area of Mumbai was the hub of cotton mills, the mill workers had a good life, with secure jobs and assured income. The mills began to shut down one after the other, in the seventies and in the eighties, due to rising costs in the city. Thousands of mill workers became jobless. Some of the mills relocated to other semi-urban locales where the cost of operations was reasonable. However the jobless workers found it difficult to relocate as other aspects of their lives like children's schools, etc were tied to the Lower Parel area. Today, many of the erstwhile mill workers live in penury; most of them have taken up odd jobs for survival.

However complex it may be, forecasting the future of a city is tough but a necessary task. Not only for policy makers, it is also important for investors and job creators to get a good sense of a city's future, such that they can take informed decisions. The first step to becoming a 'smart city' is to have a good understanding of the human and intellectual capital assets. Smart city initiatives, to be successful, will have to retain human centricity, as only evidence-based decisions will help fuel innovation, growth, and prosperity.

Countries and cities need to compete with each other quite like the way product manufacturers compete with each other. This often happens without a structured process. It is very important to adopt a proper method to showcase a city's competitive advantage, because at the end of the day it is about people and their future; it is about humans.

Smart cities are not about IT, but about people.

Synthesizing Data

Globally big data analytics is the talk of the town and is the process of examining large datasets to uncover hidden patterns, unknown correlations, market trends, customer preferences and other useful business information. At a city or country level, one needs to go one step further. Such data needs to be synthesized. In data synthesis, one puts together the separate parts that have already been analyzed with other ideas or concepts to form something new or original.

The 3P Method can not only be used to develop something privately like Powerhouse, which can bring about socio-economic change, but it can also be used by public bodies as effectively to bring about positive change within a particular geographic area. Data synthesis during the Ponder stage is critical in such initiatives.

Cities are what they are because of its people; its intellectual capital. It is pertinent that cities align development goals with its intellectual strengths. A good understanding of the prevailing innovation ecosystem helps policy makers in prioritizing policy and in sending out the right signals to investors and job creators.

Cities are often burdened with tons of good data. Synthesis helps convert that data into actionable data. Such data is

The Rich Labourer

key for real estate developers and investors in predicting demand and to identify market opportunities. The flip side is a demand-supply mismatch leading to thousands of citizens unable to get a house for themselves.

Globally universities have been accepted as the hub of research and innovation. Plus, they are in the forefront of creating a job force. Mapping the research and innovation ecosystem becomes a very valuable tool for job creators to take informed decisions about where to locate their centres. Few cities have used the link between research capacity and economic prosperity.

Those involved in the conceptualization of smart cities need to understand where economic prosperity and innovation will emerge from. Universities and innovation hubs emanate huge data as well as human capital and go on to enhance a city's brand. Bengaluru is today known as the IT capital of India. IT majors in the city get the best of talents from universities in and around Bengaluru.

It is well understood that universities create jobs and demand for real estate, attract research talent and stir up the economy beyond the campus boundaries. What is clearly not understood is the central role played by universities in the innovation ecosystem, and thus often remain an untapped resource. Universities contribute much more than being large employers themselves; they churn out talented workers and often act as innovation incubators. With international collaborations, universities connect its talent pool to the best thinkers in the world and allow access to the latest ideas from around the world. Universities contribute far more to a city's long-*run* economic prosperity than just being a stable and large employer.

Organisations and people want to know where the next Bengaluru will emerge as India continues to be a global IT leader. Synthesis of available data helps to find such answers.

Indian states are going all out to market themselves as good investment destinations. They are competing against each other for investments in fields like information technology and tourism. It is crucial that a state's policies and their planning frameworks are aligned with the state's research strengths within its universities, as well as with the qualitative and quantitative data of its human capital. Such alignment can pave the way towards confident investment and development strategies because they are based on an understanding of why a state thrives and what is in store in the future.

State leaders who go all out to promote a state or a region have a much better chance of achieving the desired results if priorities are shaped by collaboration between city, university, and business stakeholders. As is important for individuals and companies, it is equally important for a city or a state to be self-aware and understand what one is good

The Rich Labourer

at. Only if a city probes and ponders, will it be able to prove to the world.

Conclusion

The 3P Method of Probe-Ponder-Prove is based on the much written about Design Thinking principles. Design is not about aesthetics but about problem solving. Design solves problems by allowing to 'think with hands' and is inherently optimistic, because it allows one to see the future by way of sketches and prototypes. This approach brings positivity and gives hope to seemingly complex problems like poverty. Adopting such tools from design for solving problems in business and in society paves the way forward to 'Design Thinking'.

At its core is the fact that the method is human centric. There is an emphasis to deeply understand the hopes and aspirations of people. Only when this is done, will sustainable solutions emerge. In conventional problem solving methods, when one is faced with a problem, the tendency is to jump quickly to a solution. The trouble with this method is that one often ends up finding a solution to a wrongly understood problem. The major departure in the

3P Method is that ample time is spent in defining the problem.

"If I had one hour to save the world, I would spend fifty-five minutes in defining the problem and five minutes to find a solution." - Albert Einstein.

The world talks much about innovation today and its importance in organisations for their survival. Cities and countries need to be innovative as well in a world without boundaries. Although the need is well understood, innovation is not something, which is all pervasive and adopted by all. Nav Qirti, of business and design consultancy Ideactio, indicates that there are three main reasons for this: Myopia, Group Thinking and Psychological Inertia.

Myopia: People, organisations and cities often fail to see beyond the immediate present. They are happy and busy with the present. When this happens, competition often pulls the rug from under the feet. Nokia failed to see the future when Blackberry came in with email access on phones, and then Blackberry failed when iPhone came with a lot more. It is thus important to look differently or **Probe**, to understand the unmet or unimagined needs of people.

Group Thinking: When the 'boss is always right', it spells trouble. Not only within organisations, but this tends to happen in industry between businesses also, when followers blindly follow a leader and then sink like the scores of failed e-commerce portals. Kingfisher Airlines sank within a very short time when they blindly followed an owner's ego without reason. **Ponder** on insights, which emerge from thinking differently, for idea generation.

Psychological Inertia: Getting stuck to a leading position of comfort can be blinding and lead to complacency. The fortunes of way too many organizations have faltered due to this attitude. Competition need not necessarily come from another organization making the same goods, but from someone who is not even making any goods. Automobile manufacturers are facing the biggest threat today from taxi aggregators like Uber and Ola, as they target 'anyone who drives', rather than 'anyone who takes a cab'. Doing things differently allows organisations to **Prove** it, by building on the work during the Probe and Ponder stages.

The 3P method gives a structured method to being innovative.

Unlike many other business planning methodologies, the 3P method is inherently human in its approach. It thus lends itself to be used by humans at an individual level as well. While organisations find it easy to adopt such processes, it is important that an approach like this is adopted at a city and regional level for the sake of a future replete with socio-economic prosperity. Planned smart

The Rich Labourer

cities will become smart only when the hopes and aspirations of its residents are well understood and policy and practice are aligned towards fulfilling such hopes and aspirations.

A move like the demonetization of higher denomination Indian currency bills in 2016, with deep impact in the lives of every Indian, appears drastic at first look. It I slikely that months of planning would have gone behind its announcement and deployment. Many living at the bottom of the pyramid were forced to become part of the formal economy, by way of Jan Dhan bank accounts and other digital platforms. With the money secure in banks, people began to save, spend less and build credit-worthiness. For this lot, becoming a part of the formal economy, holding bank accounts and plastic money, gave them a high that they had not experienced before. They felt empowered. They felt richer. Despite expected initial hiccups, the move substantiates that it is all about humans; about their emotions and their aspirations.

Let us be human centric. Probe and ponder, before proving.

Acknowledgements

First and foremost, we would like to thank you for having read this book. We hope you had some moments of inspiration. The virtues of co-creation are many, like we have written in the previous pages. We now welcome you to share your feedback, so that we can have an updated version. You may use the following link for leaving your feedback: www.parthajeet.com/TheRichLabourer/

Next, we would also like to thank those who bought the earlier published book "Smart Phones Dumb People?" and made it popular, especially amongst the youth. That helped us progress onto this second book that you have just read. If "The Rich Labourer" does well, you will hear from us again. If not, there's always something interesting to watch on National Geographic.

Thanks to all our past clients, from whom we have learned. It is the fulfilling work we have done with such clients which have allowed us to dispense such learnings in the form of this book today. This is with the clear exception of the Oldendorff India team, the only mean and unfair client we met in over two decades. Still, we learnt.

The Rich Labourer

We are also grateful to the team at Ideactio Singapore, especially Nav Qirti, with whom we work regularly on strategic consultancy for clients. Those joint efforts have helped put a structure to our thoughts about the learnings from the past two decades and inspired us to dispense them in the form of this book.

www.ingramcontent.com/pod-product-compliance
Lightning Source LLC
Chambersburg PA
CBHW061439180526
45170CB00004B/1477